AS DARKNESS FALLS

an anthology of poetry, prose, essays, & short stories

300 SOUTH MEDIA GROUP

NEW YORK

INTRODUCTION

When my friend and fellow writer, Emily James suggested to me the theme for a new anthology, I wasn't really sure how it would be received by the writing community. I soon found out. Writers wanted and needed a platform to release their experienced unhappy endings.

As Darkness Falls became that vessel.

64 writers from around the world contributed their spilled ink to help form the finished product. Their words were not censored, the text was left the way they wrote it--the way it was intended--including different country spellings for common words.

As Darkness Falls is an anthology encompassing the stories and experiences of loss, grief, betrayal, and the reality of living within those shadows. It is a look at the darker side of life from the eyes of writers and poets who understand not everything holds a happy ending.

It is important to note, some of the stories contain raw language as well as situations and struggles that may go unseen by most--but is all too real for those who have experienced it.

We present to you As Darkness Falls—a collection of poetry, prose, and short stories.

Jay Long

300 South Media Group

TABLE OF CONTENTS

AUTHORS

To all those who find light in the darkness—shine on.

EMILY JAMES

WHEN DARKNESS FALLS

Where do you go when darkness falls?
When life gets too heavy
When your demons start to call
Where do you go when your soul searches for peace?
When your mind is slowly breaking
Your body aching for release
Do you go down the rabbit hole?
Building your home in the dark
Do you surrender to the madness?
Do you break your own heart?
Can you find a way out of the shadows?
Before they swallow you whole?
Can you find the will to go on?
Or has life taken its toll?

Emily James

HAUNTED

Maybe I've always been haunted
Just one whisper away from complete darkness
Feeling things no one else feels
Seeing things no one else sees

My world isn't black and white
I walk the staggered lines of gray
I don't want to feel these things
I don't want to see these things
Shadows dancing just out of sight
I don't want to be this person

The smile is fake
The nightmares are real
The sadness overwhelming
And I'm just one whisper away

Emily James

STARTING AGAIN

It's starting again
The whispering in my ear
Demons dancing in my mind
Repeating my every fear
It's lonely here in this darkness
A broken mirror my only friend
Shattered glass litters the floor
No one is with me in the end
I hear music playing softly
Thunder rolls across the sky
I never wanted it to be like this
I'm just too damn tired to try
Please don't let them forget me
Don't let me go in vain
Remember me in better times
I just needed to stop the pain

Emily James

Jessica Miller

SURVIVAL

Occasionally,
I find myself wanting to disappear.
Not because I hate my life
But everywhere I go
I'm blindsided by memories
I don't want to remember.
I hear your ghost screaming in my ear
That I'm worthless and will never make it.
And I have to wonder,
If you would burn
From the smoldering ashes of the past
I left on the road a few miles back
When you find out
That I rose from the hell you put me through,
A phoenix,
Bold as the sun radiating in the middle of a hot July summer…
Cool as the midnight air on an autumn night in October.
Would it kill you to know that I survived?

Jessica Miller (Rediscovery Of Wonder)

WAR PAINT

Last night, I killed you…
With words, the sharpest steel swords,
And a knight in shining armor, on a majestic white horse.
I wanted you to feel the way you made me feel
Worthless dirt; as if no one ever cared.
I died inside that day
When you first laid hands on me
I'll never forget
The day you held a gun to my head -
Painted war scenes on the walls of my mind.
I just want these memories to fade
And this war paint to dry.
So now... it's my turn…
I often murder you with poetry…
I don't write for you; I write for me
So I can set myself free, forgive myself,
And maybe learn how to live again.

Jessica Miller (Rediscovery Of Wonder)

FORGIVENESS

Forgiveness is hard. That's the part of growing up that they forget to tell you.

Forgiveness is hard. They should have told me that, the day I lost my Mother.

Forgiveness is hard. Why didn't they tell me that the day I was molested in a Conservative Mennonite church?

Forgiveness is hard. That's the one thing nobody told me when I left the church, only to find out they hated me for speaking up.

Forgiveness is hard. I should have been there for you Dad. I guess that's the part where I found out I wasn't alone all these years, after all.

Forgiveness is hard. It must be lovely to sit in the pews and pray in the churches, like you haven't killed a thousand souls.

Forgiveness is hard. I should have seen it coming. The lights. The noise. The bruises colliding with my soul and leaving me shattered as if I were a glass girl from another world.

Forgiveness is hard. I knew I should have recognized the demon in your eyes the night you held a gun to my head. I have seen that same demon before, disguised as the church. I just didn't think you would be the same.

Forgiveness is hard. They should have told me that the day I lost my children.

Forgiveness is hard. At least, that's what they say when you're sitting in the Therapists office on West Moreno Avenue.

Forgiveness is hard. If only they had told me they hated me when I first came home to make things right, I never would have bothered them again.

Forgiveness is hard. I think that's what I heard when I was told by my family for years I was going to hell and wasn't welcome because I wouldn't come back to the church. It's such a shame the preacher's daughter is the black sheep.

Forgiveness is hard. I almost forgot I made an actual life for myself while piecing myself back together, and painting rainbows of hope all over my sky since the day my life was turned around without your help.

Forgiveness is hard. Isn't that what they say while my name rolls off their tongues and lands in Gossip Square? It must be exhausting to keep up the charade of niceties to my face, turning their backs on what's really happened within four white walls and faces stained with pain. I'm afraid all I have left are these ashes, and a Phoenix rising through the smoke.

- Regrets, Forgiveness, and Scars To Last A Lifetime -

Jessica Miller (Rediscovery Of Wonder)

LYSSA DAMON

DADDY

I remember that you smelled of Aqua Velva.

All the Doris Day movies we watched together. How proud you were of your two girls and the tiny baby boy that arrived 13 years after the eldest. Stories about when you were young.

A home filled with dolls, cats, Mom's piano students, and books. Always books. From Isaac Asimov to Readers Digest.

I don't remember exactly how old I was when I met the you I didn't recognise; the one that smelled of stale smoke and alcohol. I didn't know what alcohol was, but I knew I hated it. The smell. The look in your eyes. At first, I hid from it. Then I couldn't.

I was 15 when it took you—a heart attack, they said. I hated you for so long. For choosing alcohol over us. For leaving me. I wasn't ready.

You've been gone for so long, missed so much. I finally understand that you didn't choose the darkness. It chased you down. You fought hard, but you lost.

I love you, Daddy.

Lyssa Damon

DARKNESS

Most days I love the dark.
The peace that brings Moon and Stars.
Sometimes the darkness grows fangs and claws
and chases me around my own head
taunting me with jagged edges.
Thoughts and memories.
some real,
some conjured by my imagination
run amok.
On those days
that the darkness holds monsters
that scratch and bite,
on those days
when I can barely breathe,
I remind myself
that darkness holds both
terror and treasure.
I can choose between
ghosts that whisper lies
and complete quiet.
Silence
is heavy with choices.
Beautiful peace or echos of pain.
Darkness is a reoccurring reminder to choose wisely

Lyssa Damon

SARAH HALL

WONDERLAND WASTELAND

If you ever want a glimpse inside my mind.
Picture rolling fields of wildflowers on fire.
Forked lightning and gentle Summer rain.
An ocean red from bleeding out the pain.
Wolves roaming wild, a full moon in the sky.
A little girl lost, alone she softly cries.

There's a forest full of magic with rainbow coloured leaves.
Wishing wells full of dreams, but only if you believe.
There's undiscovered beauty ready to be dug up, tombstones in a
graveyard dedicated to those whom I once loved.
There is music beating loudly, drowning out my thoughts.
Splattered words sprayed everywhere in the form of graffiti art.
There's a devil and an Angel. Sometimes it's hard to tell them apart.
There's mayhem, and there's madness and monsters lurking in the
dark.

My mind is fantasy mixed with beauty and a splash of the colour
dark.
It's Wonderland mashed with Neverland and a Wasteland all in one.

Sarah Hall

THE LONG DARK ROAD

I know it's been a long dark road to finding yourself,
and to discovering all of the true authentic beauty
deep within that damaged soul.

I know it's been a long dark road travelled
to understanding all that you can
and will ever be,
a path walked neither
easily or comfortably.

I know it's been a long dark road
to accepting yourself
exactly as you are
and that loving yourself,
has come at the highest price
of trauma, adversity
and unimaginable sacrifice.

I know it's been a long dark road
of falling down and scraping knees.
Digging deep inside
for strength as fuel,
just to keep that fire
burning inside of you.

I know it's been a long dark road
of seeking light
at the end of the tunnel.
A trail left behind you,

of bleeding hope from your heart.
A lifetime of anguish and pain
and collecting scars
along the way.

I know it's been a long dark road
of releasing all those tears
that you've cried,
wondering if you will ever make it out
of the fucking darkness alive.

I know it's been a long dark road
to a home that is your own,
where your soul can find peace
and your wings can now unfurl.

I know it's been a long dark road
to a place you are free to fly.

Rest now,
my darling.

For you have finally arrived.

Sarah Hall

MY DARKEST HOUR

I howled. Guttural and visceral.

Until it burned like fire in the back of my throat and my lungs could no longer exhale, or my voice make any noise.

I howled with piercing screams of hopelessness.

Sounds of a lost, terrified child. Muted amongst the noise, in a bustling crowd of strangers, who never stopped or noticed.

I howled with the anguish of a person in mourning.

Buckled over by pain and slowly staggering. Consumed by my grief whilst inconsolable in my suffering.

I howled for my worth and for what I deserved.

For the sacrifices I have made. For the bottomless pit inside my being, drowning in my loneliness.

I howled.
To be seen.
To be felt.
To be known.
To be heard.
And to be touched.

I howled like a ferocious storm.

Swirling and squalling.
Tearing up the ocean as it heads towards the shore.

I howled for those who never howled for me.

As Darkness Falls

For a safe place in this world where I can breathe and bleed.

I howled with the longing of a trapped and ghosted soul.

Stuck between the realms of eternity and immortality, eternally condemned, never to be set free.

I howled for my numb and empty heart.

I howled for my future, and I howled for my past.

In my darkest hour of my darkest day.

I howled for me.
I howled for you.
I howled for us.
I howled for love.

Sarah Hall

TAVARES BOWLEG

THE FALL OF NIGHT

The sky darkens, and night falls around my face.
The crisp breeze of the night bellows against
the harsh heat of the sky king.
The symphony of the night explodes
as its nocturnal orchestra awakens the bastard Prince of the sky.
He smiles down on his loyal subjects,
bathing them in a still comforting glow:
a glow that make(s) his subjects seem alien
with eyes a shine and a shadow that moves
independently of their master.
As night falls, the barrier between the worlds weaken
and creatures of myth legend and memories long forgotten walk.
Walk just out of view adhering like a spider to the corner of the eye.
When night falls in all her passionate beauty.
embracing the earth like a new lover.
When night falls, I weep for morning and her sky king the sun comes;
they come with the winged sandals of Hermes.
I weep for morning, and her sun king quickens my sleeps,
night falls and slips through my fingers
the harsh laser beams of sky king burns through my nightly fortress
raiding the orchestra and banishing the denizens
of the Princes' Kingdom to its other worldly dimension
eyes dull, and shadows are shackled to their master.
The assault of morning and her sky king

As Darkness Falls

beat against the windows to my soul
and I struggle to hold on to the last wisps of night
but I struggle in vain for morning
and her king's army of light batters at my fortress,
they break into every corner of Nights Kingdom.
The Sun Kings lasers punch relentlessly at night
and as night falls and morning comes in her chariot of light
I.........................awake

Tavares Bowleg

NICOLE LABONTE

YOU ARE DARKNESS

You are the darkness that I was born to know; my biggest betrayer, cursed for your sins, I walk the earth with the weight of your mistakes.

You are my darkness; your face haunts me, your words whispering into my ear, hushed like a ghost but so loud in my head, screaming unwanted, unlovable. An innocent child; brought into the world by an affair, just a bastard you chose to create, a flaw in your plan for the perfect life. My face was his face. You saw it as you ripped me from his arms, my loving father, never to be seen again.

You are my darkness; your betrayals dug so deep the wounds still raw and bleeding they cannot heal. I am still that little girl searching for her mother, the one that ran away on your never-ending search for happiness, abandoning, cursing as you walked out the door. When you finally returned, no apologies, no shame. Four years, you vanished while your offspring suffered at the hands of a man you knew to be abusive.

You are the darkness that I know, the darkness that I will always know; it lives inside of me. I carry your burdens, with chains around my ankles, keeping me anchored to the ground; it gets hard to breathe. You left me here, never able to escape the life you gave to me when all I crave is stability, normalcy.

As Darkness Falls

You are darkness. Light will never touch you; you're too far to reach. You stole my childhood that I deserved to have. You kept me from the man that wanted me. Did you enjoy knowing that I went to visit his grave? Did it eat at you the way it ate at me, knowing he was gone?

You are darkness; you are betrayal. I am better now, I chose to walk away this time, and I will never look back.

Nicole Labonte

APRIL Y. SPELLMEYER

I AM GRIEF

grief is not affected by time for the living the ones left behind – the rawness and sting of a wound that will never heal never to scar – grief is a bit of a diva and never stands in the shadows for long – it is always there to remind me of the day it came and unpacked itself in my life – it has left bits of haze and grey – fading the once vibrant colors in my world – it rips out memories with a smell – a sound – a feeling to bring me to my knees – the taste of bitterness grief has laced on my tongue never able to swallow it whole – grief force-feeds bits and pieces – even to this day i choke on a tsunami of what-ifs, could-haves, should-haves – destroying the walls i built – grief takes control leaving me helpless to tread in a sea of emotional torment – at times, i wish I could drown – my battle with grief has become a lost cause – it has drained my strength – it has made me weak – i am unable to be the rock everyone expects me to be – i wave my white banner – I surrender – i have become grief

April Y. Spellmeyer

THE FORGOTTEN GIRL

nobody knows who the forgotten girl is
she is the one who is a hazy memory
nobody keeps her around for too long
she is a wisp of smoke from a blown
out candle but she still takes the risk
and wears her heart upon her sleeve
even though she knows
it will be flayed open time and again
she weeps as she sews her wounds
and the scars from the past
with bruised fingertips
her words linger on the tip of her tongue
her words denied breath
and she swallows the decay
filling her throat with filthy bitterness
as much as she denies it
she knows who she is
because nobody ever hears
nobody ever sees
nobody ever loves
nobody ever remembers
the forgotten girl

April Y. Spellmeyer

DAWN P. HARRELL

ENVELOPING DREAD

It visits from time to time
That slowly enveloping dread
I tell myself I know who I am but that doubt
covers me in an oily puddle
Makes the strongest unsure when it lays your soul bare
seemingly for all to see
Would I ever find a way to beat it
I wonder would I miss the haunting
Or finally find a way to rest within this skin

Dawn P. Harrell

DESTRUCTION OF ME

I can barely remember what made me think you loved me
Seems like there had to be happy before it got so wrong
The nights I prayed the sun would hurry
The ones I prayed you'd sleep all night
It's taken so long to rest with both eyes closed
To relearn that my memories can be trusted
To know the monster isn't really me
The words that broke me over and over
are changing from screams to whispers in my head
So tired
Yet every day I wake up it's a little lighter
Since you're gone
The destruction of me is reversing in slow but sure ways
I may not put my heart in the hands of another
But I can like me
And on good days, see why others might too
Now that I'm free
All my physical wounds are long gone
It's the ones inside that still bleed
But I'm slowing the flow every day I make it through

Dawn P. Harrell

ASTRID S.

HOLDING MY BREATH

Today I looked up how long it would take
to die holding my breath.
Today I looked up how long it would take
to die holding my BREATH!
The hardest thing that I tried to do
as a competition when I was a kid with a friend,
but now not as a competition with a friend,
but with my lungs.

How long can I hold my breath
before I can't hold my breath any longer?

How long until my lungs give out?

Today I stood in front of a window,
and imagined what it would be like
to glide through the air like a bird.
No, I didn't.
I imagined what it would be like
to run into the outside,
away from the frame that caged me inside,
to go from the 10th story
all the way down to the concrete,
My better judgement said
it wouldn't be a very pretty sight
if someone I cared about found me,
that's the voice
that sings a song 24/7 on

As Darkness Falls

Replay.
Replay..
Replay...

It wouldn't be fair to a stranger either
or the child that is walking with his mother
just wanting to go to the candy store.

So I suffer quietly
with only the song in my head
And wait for life
to finish its course
and hoping
that it will finish soon
because I am done.

I am tired,

I quit.

Astrid S.

THE VOICES IN MY HEAD

Having anxiety and depression
is like being exhausted and terrified
all at the same time.
It's me wanting to do something,
but having no desire
to get anything done.
It's wanting to make friends,
but not wanting to talk to anyone.
It's craving no noise,
but not being left alone
to drown in the silence.
But I sit there,
on my bed
waiting for someone to notice
that I am gone,
but knowing no one knows me,
disappointing myself again.
and eventually, I find a cigarette lighter
touch it oh so gently to my leg;
flame burning away skin.
Someone walks in.
They comfort me in the moment
and I think I have a friend
But then after the party
they forget who I am.
So I take the lighter to my wrist,
burning away the skin until it hurts
I go to the kitchen,
grab the butcher knife.
Cut deep into my skin,
collapse on the floor

As Darkness Falls

Surrounded by my favorite things
Yet least favorite things
Noise,
People,
Accomplishment...
Disappointment.
So I die sad
and happy

It's always mixed feelings

Astrid S.

GRACEFULLY BROKEN

THE MONSTER THAT YOU CREATED IN ME

When I was a kid, I'm always curious of what does the monster looks like. I always wanted to see if they are as ugly and scary as what we've seen in movies, story books and how our elders describe them in bedtime stories. Out of little curiosity, I continue to look for answers about the appearance of a real monster. I keep on gathering evidence from videos, documentaries, newspapers and still hoping to meet one but those different evidence's thirst me for more knowledge. Questions and desires became visible when you came but then walked out in my life.

My blurry vision of that monster turns clearly. All the pain and sufferings you brought into my life made me who I am today, a scary giant monster waiting to come out and punish you.

Every day I am struggling to get rid of these frightening thoughts and plans that are keeping me awake at night. I fought so hard against this monster, but defeat is what I always got. It made me do things averse to my will. It drives me insane and impatient. It is exhausting pushing me to torture you. It is very compelling. I wanted to utter it to acquire my revenge and let you feel every day. I ought you to realize the destruction that you have created in me. The chaos and nightmares that you tied in me lead this darkness to fill my emptiness.

Now, I am still confined in the dark. Shadows and nightmares are guarding my soul. Walls are becoming higher and darker. It is blinding me. It is depriving me of reaching the horizon. I am struggling to get out. The doors are shutting down. The windows are locked. The keys are unavailable, and I cannot move. I think I am indulging in the dark, the darkness in me. I am becoming a monster that I once want to see. The monster that you created in me.

Gracefully Broken

CHARLENE ANN BENOIT

EMPTY SHARDS OF BROKEN

Time stopped the day you left;
there was no going back,
no moving forward,
just an excruciating moment
stuck forever on repeat.
I was there
when you took your last breath,
kissed your forehead
as your skin
grew forever cold.
I cannot unlove you,
nor can I forget your face.
The hopes and dreams and plans,
have become nothing more
than empty shards of broken.
I cut myself
each and every time I try to move.
My love and guilt both keep me here,
clinging to you,
to your memory.

Charlene Ann Benoit

MIRROR

"I look at you,
I see the lines life left laying on your face."
"You, you couldn't do anything the easy way, could you?
"It was your actions that brought me to this place."
"How many tears have I cried because of you?"
"How many times have I hung my head in shame?"
"You had love for everyone else but me,
all you gave to me was blame."
"Taking pieces one at a time,
you've left me empty more often than not."
"You offered to others what I couldn't afford,
sacrificing dreams that I had sought."
"There are days when I can't stand the sight of you,
when you fill my heart with hate."
"Do you know how badly your betrayal broke me?"
"It was you that left me in this state."
"You made me the casualty of your ignorance."
"My life is the product of your insecurities and fear."
"Now I have to rebuild everything that you have broken"...
things I tell myself while looking in the mirror.

Charlene Ann Benoit

SPENSER SPELLMEYER

BATTLEFIELD

We are the soldiers who march upon a blood-stained battlefield. Our brothers and sisters dead at our feet with their dark clones beside them. We are the soldiers who march through the day just to say "I'm fine" with the many lies we have already spoken. We suture our wounds with barbed wire and rusty nails. But the only damage you see is a little cut when we are aligned with scars. We are taken as a joke by you calling us "freaks" or "attention seekers". You tell us to "just be happy" or "you're just sad" when it's more than that. You silence us with your ignorance and childish deeds. You cause the most amount of pain by not letting us scream out. We hope someone hears, but you suffocate our cries with your deafened ears.

Spenser Spellmeyer

CRISTINA LANE

HOW MANY

How many times did I catch you in a lie?
How many times did you continue to deny?
How many times did you tell me to leave if I wasn't happy?
How many times did I walk out that door?
How many times did I come back, and what for?
How many night did I cry myself to sleep?
How many nights did you make me sleep alone?
How many chances did you think I would give?
How many times have you regretted losing me?

Cristina Lane

BIZARRE MIZZ WILLIAMS

TABLE OF LIFE

*I wanna spin a tale of a soul near worn away, one that didn't cheat but played for keeps in people's mindless games. Don't sit too close, boy; I just might bite. I belong to that time between dusk and dawn because the day is too bright. I never needed no man to bring me the sunshine, my eyes could be blind, and I'd still wear my shades at night. Besides, I already got it on my grind, my own brilliant and familiar sunrise. I've been known to stash it in my pocket, keep it locked up in my wallet like I bought it until it's my turn to shine. As darkness falls and they begin to seek the fading light, it's me that *sets fire to* the tables in this game called life, where you have the nerve sit and feast your eyes, but you fold, where's your ace in the hole now? You can barely watch me hold it down when I throw the dice. You can't leave a mark like mine; I ignite the night like I shot a sparkler into the sky. Play at your own risk in my casino. Make a bet you won't regret. Before you place it, don't forget, I don't need a damn thing to get me through until tomorrow except the beat that plays in the back of my head. I let the hustle drown my sorrow, and when it gets too dark to see, it's me that takes the stars out of the sky, and I hang them up like morning light.*

Bizarre Mizz Williams

FEAR IN FIFTY FORMS

*I admit I'm not the gentlest girl to ever become a mother. I was raised
in the woods with mama, daddy, and four older brothers.*
We lived off the land, and as the youngest, they taught me best.
*Learning to survive that way wasn't wicked, but still there was no
rest.*
From sun up to sundown, yep, just like they say.
There wasn't a single thing in the dark that I hadn't seen by day.
*I never learned fear, and until junior high, I thought everyone lived
like this.*
*We had love, but we were poor...unaware of what "they" wouldn't
miss.*
*I fought though, as hard as I could, never surrendering my ways to
them.*
*Took them all by surprise when they finally realized that my knees
wouldn't bend.*
Yes, a country girl could survive anything; of this I was so sure.
Fifty forms of fear and hardship I had pioneered and would endure.
*I grew tired of the judgement and quit high school in 12th grade that
very 1st week.*
*A year later, I was in college for Business and English, having aced
my GED.*
*I was proud of my integrity; not a single person I'd met was quite like
me.*
But all too soon I became a mother, and I never got that degree.
If I went back, the Dean would see my 4.0s and grant me my mistake.
Oh brave I was for there's not a mold I would not go on to break.
*But life changes, and we make time for the things that we can not live
without.*
Teaching children to survive this crazy world, to this I am devout.
*After my oldest was born, his daddy died, and the first strike of fear
came into my heart.*

It dawned on me that there are things you can not control, and it's more difficult without a partner.

Without the faintest of my own acknowledgement another man came into my life.
We had three more kids, two girls and a boy, and one day I became his wife.
We struggled long to bring peace to our family and make things as they should.
Seems now that you don't learn everything growing up in the woods.
Where once I feared no hell from this great big world around.
I began to question if my dying day my children would be safe and sound.
I used to wake up and go to sleep with a clean conscience, I never had a care.
But now, as darkness falls, I whisper urgently my final prayers.
"Lord, please look over mine, and if it should be time for them to go...keep them in your arms...or take me instead...please just call us all home.

I did my best to show them love and right from wrong and keep them free from sin, survival is all I had, to each this mama would gladly pay their debt in the end. Amen."

Bizarre Mizz Williams

TABASSUM HASNAT

THE GRIT TO GRIEF

It did take a lot of grit
to grief the loss
of what had been of
utmost gravity in your life,
yet it was vital to let go
of a few bits of valor
here and there to once again
validate that life goes on
with or without whatsoever
you valued the most
or the littlest.

Tabassum Hasnat

THE DOWNFALL OF MY DARKNESS

There had been a time,
when I stealthily stood beside
the half-drawn blinds, clenching
and unclenching both of my fists,
with lids livid with languish;
as I stared at the searing serenity,
of the very early streaks of the sun,
whilst wishing how wondrous
it would have been if those selfsame
streaks seeped into my insides;
slaying those shards of darkness
damnably dwelling right within me.
And now be the beholder of mine,
as I once again tiptoed my way
to those half-drawn blinds, slightly
slouching against the window pane,
with fists, no longer clenched or unclenched,
relishing in the reverie of my insides,
that no longer remained enslaved
to those enervating episodes of
one maleficent melancholy,
whilst the sun set the horizon
ablaze with its raging rays;
And that was how, while often
floundering and falling in the abyss,
of nothingness, I sustained holding
onto something, be it anything;

As Darkness Falls

for I knew there lingered dews,
of hope midst the downpour of
hopelessness;
for I knew there lingered
one daunting darkness before,
every divinely devised dawn.

Tabassum Hasnat

DISTRESS & DURABILITY

*Every distress shall
only enhance every
bit of our durability
as every other pain
of ours shall be that
only power to propel
us further,
be it with those steps
that at times faltered,
and at times remained
firm, solely to suspire,
survive and to sustain.*

Tabassum Hasnat

MANDY KOCSIS

FIGHTING WARS

Days like today, I have to remind myself that I fought for this life.
I mean, clawed-my-fingers-bloody,
Do-anything-to-survive,
Ride-meets-die,
FOUGHT for this fucking life.
That there was a time in my life
When THIS life was the fairytale
I was surviving for.

Hindsight, 2020
Years after the war was over
Just a haunted battlefield
Even ghosts fear to tread
Where memories are bloody
And the nights are hell-bent

I realize how much easier it was
To fight a war
At least one of us wanted to survive.

Mandy Kocsis

EVIL CAN'T WIN

Pounding on each door you pass
Screaming down the hall
Blood flowing like a river
You slip, you slide, you fall
You glance behind you quickly
At the monsters getting close
Evil voices fill the air
Screaming, twisted ghosts
You know if they catch you
You'll die screaming; you'll die slow
You know they'll drain you dry, again
Then try to steal your soul
Your heart is pounding loudly
Nearly drowning out the sounds
Of bloody, soulless terror
That, EVERYWHERE, abounds
Now you're running blindly
As the evil ghosts give chase
There HAS to be an exit
Out of this Hell-bound place
Flying 'round the corner
You spot way up ahead
A square of blessed hope
Yet your soul is filled with dread
You know you'll never make it
It's too far down the hall
Then bloody bones snatch at your hair

As Darkness Falls

And you begin to fall
Into a light so blinding
No darkness can exist
And you realize that your running
Would always end like this
A period to a sentence
A stone upon a grave
But at least you went down swinging
With every step you ever made
And you know it counts for something
Now that it's finally done
You gave your all and faltered
Yet, somehow, you still won.

Mandy Kocsis

THE DARKEST REACHES

I was born beyond the stars
In the darkest reaches of a lover's heart
Meant to shine so others see
Darkness isn't a bad thing to be
It's how you let it mold your soul
How it fills your broken whole
That's where the difference goes
I've lived for years within the light;
I killed myself to make it right
Once back in darkness, I came to see
I was born to set love free
And there's so much more to all of me.

Mandy Kocsis

EVA COFFEY

ACCEPTANCE

I'm so afraid, my love.
I'm afraid to live this life without you in it.
You were my motivation, my inspiration, my muse.
I don't want to be lost, but I am. I am.
You're gone. I'm hopelessly bereft.
You were the voice of reason, my pillar of strength.
And losing you means losing my very essence as well.
My world has never been so silent.
So still.
So devoid of warmth.
I'm missing you with every labored breath.
Now I live in a vacuum that I can't control.
It scares me to the very core.
I'm afraid because now I fear life.
For life has suddenly become so empty.
For life can no longer give me peace anymore.
I lost my sunrise, my sunset, my moonlight.
I lost my home when I lost you.
My pain is mine to keep.
All mine to feel.
No way to cure.
No way to ease.
So, I'll carry it inside my heart until the end of time.

Till I walk beside you once again with your warm, large hand in mine.
I'm making peace with my sadness.
I'm learning how to deal with your absence.
I realize that my life has changed. Irrevocably.
I've accepted that I have to live with a void that will always be there.
One breath at a time.
One step at a time.
I move forward with humble gratitude as each new day brings me closer to you.

Eva Coffey

IN THIS HEART

Within this heart
there is a huge gaping hole
of nothingness
And I'm standing at this precipice
trying to resist the beautiful siren call
of the dark, cold abyss of oblivion
This absence of feeling you
wounds me even deeper
than the barrenness of your touch
How I crave you in wild rage
for even a single rush
Oh, my darling
Oh, my forever love
Never could I imagine
that I would terribly miss you
this very much
I will get used to you being gone
But I will never get used to not needing you
I will want you, long for you, and ache for you
Until life dissipates away from my body
I will carry this pain, this tortured agony, with all my dignity
This world is not the world that I knew anymore
Life has no significant meaning for me
Losing you means losing myself
I'm now merely existing
While drowning in sweet memories and dreams
As I miss you with every labored breath

As Darkness Falls

I force myself how to make do and survive
I strive to make every moment count
For I believe that one day, I will find myself back
Safe and warm in your loving arms

Eva Coffey

SURRENDER

It'll be two years exactly this summer.
Numbing and choosing to be alone is my way of coping right now.
Like living in a bubble or rather a glass cage.
I refuse to let anything destroy this modicum of peace that I've
painstakingly built since you've been gone.
It's the only way to give sense to my life.
It's the only way for me to survive without breaking up in pieces.
I'm still struggling with your passing.
There are times, I can't even wrap my mind that you're no more here.
It's surreal.
As if, this is all a dream.
A recurring nightmare that I can't just wake up from.
Sometimes in the middle of the night,
I feel an emptiness so palpable that it cuts so deep,
wounding my very core.
And all I can do is let my heart bleed, again and again.
Saying your name in silent agony like a mantra of sanity.
No matter what I do to forget this grief inside of me,
it will still live on.
In every nook and cranny of my mind, of my heart and of my soul.
Profoundly imprinted within me like an invisible scar caused by the
burning of this tragic loss.
I have accepted your death.
I deal with your absence every day.
I don't feel you like how I used to anymore.
I'm not sharing your pain anymore.
My body feels so hollow, and my heart aches in continue.

Loneliness…
Another feeling that I'll have to carry within me until I see you once again.
I'm in surrender.
Living from moment to moment.
As I fight my way through this incessant turbulent of needs.
Of wanting you.
Of needing you.
Of missing you.
Oh… so terribly.
Your love…
That wondrous and unconditional love.
It still warms my soul and my whole entire being.
I can still feel it coursing through my veins.
I cling tightly onto it to keep this torturous sadness at bay.
It makes being lonesome, bearable in a certain way.
As I stand here, all alone facing another new day.
Without you.

Eva Coffey

NICOLE CARLYON

EMPTY ROOMS

I went searching for you again today
Through empty corridors
empty rooms
I close my eyes
and if only for a moment
I pretend
that your arms are wrapped around me
My face is buried
in your chest
I inhale
I exhale
Alone again
Missing you

Nicole Carlyon

BLUE SKY DREAMING

There are days when I sit outside
Surrounded by nothing but the sky and my breath calm and slow
I am fighting a war with the voices in my head,
and today they may not be winning
But I fear
tomorrow I may not get to sit under this blue sky
and listen to this heartbeat of mine
Pulse steady
I fear tomorrow I let the war inside me win

Nicole Carlyon

THERE HAS TO BE MORE

Today I stare at the sky and I try and talk with you
I feel so alone in the world
Nothing makes sense
My head is spinning
Words keep doing somersaults
My mind is a mess
I just need to feel your presence
A tender touch
To make me feel less out of place
In my world which is full of chaos
An existence that makes me feel second best
I sigh as the emptiness engulfs me
A scream stuck in my throat
Tears flowing freely
I want to run to a place free from noise
Where I can sit in silence and no longer hide
From this world that has never understood me
Where I can be free to do more than just survive

Nicole Carlyon

T H SMART

INDIFFERENCE

Numbness settling like morning dew
drugging the senses and fraying nerves.
No desire to sit and none to stand.
Sapping strength from all reserves –
Indifference

Whichever way will do just fine.
Shoulders shrugged selflessly
trusting another to lead
wherever they care to go –
Indifference

Lack of feeling, no need, no want.
Energy drained from every cell.
Motivation but part of history.
This body feels like an empty shell –
Indifference

The treat of a tear but taints the eye
Even heartache is a powerless find.
Welcomed weakness, in this dark
impenetrable void shrouds the mind –
Indifferent …

T H Smart

BLAZING ANGER

Blood boils and veins freeze
anger grips the beating heart
silent tongue and painted smile
and eyes throw a flaming dart
Anger, rages like a wild dog caught.
Held in traps set by selfish men,
men to whom this is but a game
played with too little care too often
Fire, blazing within the belly
Will not be contained for long
embers will burn paths to freedom
if this charade should carry on.
Burn, ever stronger still.
Flames fueled by careless words
feasting on senseless sayings leaving
smoke damage and deep wounds.
Glow, cinders tell your tale.
Smoldering ashes set the scene
of hearts and minds scorched and smoky hue
Damaged, charred, wasted, uncleaned.

T H Smart

CONFLICTING LOVE

Seduced and stroked by gentle words.
Shattered by the same.
One moment, warm and loving,
the next, the cruelest game.

A heartfelt invitation given.
The coldest rejection followed.
The surface full and charming,
but the inside proved only hollow.

The smile, the laugh slightly teasing.
The voice hiding a storm's revolt!
A sudden change, no warning,
and again, at my door, cast the fault.

In an instant, this tempest forgotten,
but the memory haunts me still.
What innocence next will fuel this rage?
It leaves me cold and fear-filled.

T H Smart

LEIGH ALISON

UNINVITED GUEST

Anxiety took up residence a long, long time ago
She can't remember a time when it wasn't always there
An uninvited guest that became a tenant who never pays rent
It's always there, and it's always lurking in the shadows of her being
It roams the cluttered hallways of her mind and adds to the noise in her head
It's in her mind, and her thoughts, and her belly, and her heart
She can feel it
She can hear it
She can taste it
It keeps track of her every move and every thought, biding its time and piercing her soul with its razor-sharp talons
Some days it's just a superficial scratch
Other days it draws blood
Oozing, seeping, and flowing
On the good days, it just gently trickles beneath the surface of her skin
On the bad days, the blood flows forth like the untempered current of a river that has burst its banks
It's out of control, and panic bubbles to the surface of the calm exterior she fights so hard to present
Those are the hardest days... the days when it takes every ounce of strength to will herself out of bed, pick up her sword and shield, put

on her war paint, and lead herself into battle
But she does it
Day in and day out
Hour in and hour out
Minute by minute
She hasn't given up
Not yet
And she's not about to

Leigh Alison

SACRIFICE

I died for you today
On a wet, cold, muddy field
Alone, yet surrounded by the dead and dying
All of us in a quest for freedom that would never be our own
Echoes of the screams and gunfire and explosions fading in my ears
The only sound that I hear now is the thudding of my heart in my
chest, and even that is fading.

I died for you today
You will never know my thoughts and dreams
Or the life I lived that was snuffed out like a candle no longer needed
to illuminate the night
You will never know the people I loved and how I did what I did for
them and for you

I died for you today
I hope it won't be in vain
My blood spilled out, mixing with the mud and rain
A sacrifice of life and love
An act of courage cloaked in fear and pain

I died for you today
And you will never even know my name

Leigh Alison

ANGEL WINGS

I drowned
In the loss of you
Treading water
With legs that were too tired to move
I sank like a stone
With the weight of your absence
Only a few days old
You were stolen from me
And gifted angel wings
You left this earth before it could scald you
You left this earth before I could shower you with my unconditional love
I looked for the signs of your anticipated arrival, but your presence had been erased before I could even get to know you
Misguided intentions of those older than I
Thinking that removing all trace of you would ease the loss of you
But they were wrong
It made the void bigger, wider, longer, deeper, emptier
I looked for signs of you in each drawer of your bureau
Opening each one to look for the tiny garments that would have been yours
But they were gone
Rushed out and discarded
Along with the crib and changing table
All disposed of before I even got released from the maternity ward
I couldn't breathe for the missing of you
My breath left my body the minute you lost yours

As Darkness Falls

I think of you every year on your birthday
And every day in between
You are in my heart
You are in my soul
But a piece of me
Died that day
The day you got your angel wings

Leigh Alison

Dedicated to Lyn and Stu Walton

For my angel sisters who I never got to meet, Angela Claire
and Catherine Dawn

LORNA HUSBAND

BREATH

You left me just like you found me
Struggling to breathe
You brought me light
You brought me life
You brought me love
But it's cold here in the shadows
The sun doesn't shine all of the time
Darkness must fall again
I guess that's why you had to go
But I still have the moon
And midnight memories
And these dreams of you
Holding me until that last breath

Lorna Husband

RUBY JANE PRIAS

SILENT PAIN

My life is full of broken pieces that people didn't usually see. They always see me as a strong and independent one, but actually, I'm not. I need someone to be with, someone who will understand me, and a shoulder to cry on. I normally cry at night and wake up in the morning like nothing happened. Life is full of unexpected happenings, and I normally get dizzy in its ride. I choose to cover up my true feelings thinking that I will surpass it. I also choose to smile to inspire the people around me, even though it hurts a lot. I choose to be strong, thinking that my tears will not fall. I learn to flow with the current, but it always alternates.

Ruby Jane Prias

MY PERSONAL BRAND OF HEROIN

"Love is like a drug; it can neither cure nor destroy you." It all started when I first noticed you; my life becomes more meaningful each day. I felt like I'm alive and cured from the previous illness I had. Each day seemed to be a year. Each darkness was surpassed by the light you created in my life, all of the pain was eased, and my life was renewed.

That day I even noticed ants and termites, all of the little and unnoticed things before, appeared in my sight. The wind whispered me your name, the thunder roared it, and the lightning wrote. What a wonderful feeling it is, even my heart was jumping, and all my tiny brain cells were thinking of you. All of my cells are working well; they are all rejoicing, making me more repaired.

From then, you became my maintenance. You perpetuate my feeling of relief and make me stronger. We enjoyed the time together, we dreamed and looked at the stars together, we walked under the heat of the sun and wait until it sets, and we promised to love each other forever. But that forever was just a concept; when I woke up one day knowing that all of the promises are gone, you started walking alone, leaving me broken.

My medicine that once cured me is now my greatest brand of heroin that destroyed my life. My body is in severe pain and unconscious due to its effect, a moment of blindness, deafness, and speechless drawn in to my world. I was totally sick and felt like dying.

Ruby Jane Prias

SUNNY WRIGHT

OMISSION

I'm afraid to die.
But I'm even more afraid to live
in a world
as ugly as this.

I'm afraid to cry.
But I'm even more afraid to smile,
look you straight in the eye
and say;

'We did a fine job.'

Yet deep inside
I knew,
we did not.

Sunny Wright

UNFORSAKEN

Should you ever find yourself.
Haunted by the remnants of your past.

Should you ever find yourself.
Moving back because you moved way too fast.

Should you ever find yourself.
Floating downstream in a river of tears.

Should you ever find yourself.
Locked in a prison of your own trembling fears.

Should you ever find yourself.
Stuck in a hole deep in the ground.

Should you ever find yourself.
In an empty room devoid of any sound.

Should you ever find yourself.
By yourself…
Promise yourself this one thing.
Find yourself...

Sunny Wright

JENNIFER JENNINGS DAVES

SIX FEET UNDER

Dishes in the sink
Piling ever higher
No one remembers
How to pay the bills
No more lights
The house is now cold and dark
No one can call
There is no phone
Bills are in piles, all left unpaid
For they all are in shock
That she left that way
Now ask yourselves this
Was it really all that hard
To help with these things
Now and again
To give her a break from the burdens of life
While she still breathed
Did you really have to have her six feet under
Before you realized how much she did
Quietly, without being told
She washed, she cleaned, she paid your bills
She kept you fed, clothed and your belly full
She gave you all her time, her energy, her love

And all you left her with was that empty shell
Now. Six. Feet. Under.

Jennifer Jennings Daves

THE MONSTER WITHIN

Was the monster without
Sneaking around under cover of dark
Hiding in plain sight
The whole world could see
But no one knew the monster
Quite like me
He smiled and laughed
He always acted so kind
But with that smile
He made many blind
Moving freely, he flattered
Showing himself honest
Among the blind
Never seeing what was in sight
For all the world to see
And no one questioned his motives
Or his collection of keys
Though no one saw them
They lay hidden in a box
Only removed when the urge to visit
To take a taste of innocence
Was a special delight
He kept his passion hidden
From the world, from his wife
All would gasp in horror
If they really knew
What lay behind the doors

All those keys went to
And maybe if that happens
The silent screams would finally stop

Jennifer Jennings Daves

KATHLEEN SCHOLMER

CONTROL

My demons within are trying to escape the depths of my soul.
The water's too deep; the cuts upon my skin take control of my heart,
keeping the darkness from submerging it in iciness.
What happens when the sun comes and dries up all the water
containing my demons?
When the darkness coats my heart with hatred and anger?
When my skin is no longer bleeding self-control of my own twisted
soul?
What happens when the only way out of this hole that I've dug myself
is a bullet to this beating heart that's been pumping blood through my
veins for 17 years?
The only things that have been keeping me sane are the ropes tying
me down in a cold surrounding.
With these demons swimming to escape my ocean,
no one is there to help me, to save me from the pain I've had to
endure.
I'm alone,
Trying my hardest to hide my demons within the depths of my ocean.

Kathleen Schlomer

GEORGE DELGADO

TRAUMA

every time i sit down
with a pen in one hand
and my heart in the other
i tightly grasp
the many traumas &entries
that keep my mind racing

wondering if i
would still be the same man
had i not faced
these struggles//

a never-ending cycle
of what-if's
that keeps my
pen on paper
and my hand from ever
letting go of this
heart i struggled
to finally get back

George Delgado

BLOOD

i never made a conscious decision to
have my life go one way or another
everything that kept my mind sane
had fallen out of place
making every single decision I made
a catalyst for the next
thus creating the inevitability
that my future would suffer
and once my failures reached
overwhelming proportions
the color of blood
was all I could see
all i could smell
it became all i knew

George Delgado

BRANDY LANE

WATER COLORED SUNSET

You boarded the plane as I tearfully
collapsed into a heap on the floor.
I stared out the window as I watched
my hopes and dreams,
all of my love for you...
taxi down the runway.

My heart pounding,
I cried out in angst at my stupidity!
How could I let this day come?
How could I let you go so easily
without telling you how I feel?

The jet made its final turn,
and engines flared to full throttle.
Racing toward the sun
as it set on the horizon,
I focused on the colors
in their pastel hues,
through my watery tears.

Brandy Lane

LIFE GOES ON

No one would miss me if I was gone...
no one would really care
they'd all forget my laughter
the way it filled the air.

They wouldn't miss my poems
however short or long
or how I sang the words
to every single song.

They wouldn't miss my cooking
or the things I baked,
or even remember eating
the cheesecakes I would make.

They won't remember the concerts
at which I used to sing,
or the games I used to play
they won't remember a thing.

Life will go on without me,
some might shed a tear..
but I bet they won't remember me
in the coming year.

You might think I'm crazy,
or maybe a little blue...
but heck, no one thinks of me now!
Admit it; you know it's true.

When's the last time you reached out
to be the first to say hello?
Go on; I'll give you a moment…
'cause I'd really like to know.

So here I sit so lonely
and all I wish I had…
is someone who really loved me
that might make me glad.

But the phone's not ringing,
or making its little chime
because no one ever thinks of me
they haven't got the time.

Brandy Lane

SPIT

I feel sick…
in the pit of my stomach;
it feels like a boulder
that I cannot get out.

I'm a conglomeration
of every mistake I've ever made.…
the fat on my thighs
my flabby muscles…

I wake in pain,
I sleep in pain,
I starve myself
then gain again.

All of the lies I took to heart.
Every deceitful act against me…
I stuffed it down.
My joints ache continuously.

All I want is the time back.
I wouldn't have blamed myself.
I wouldn't have listened to the naysayers.
I would have worked harder.

It seems like every time I move the obstacles,
more would pile on…
like sand in a pit
constantly trying to level itself.

My right knee then left
then neck, then hip,
my elbow.
Oh, the headaches.

I danced as hard as I could
when I was young
trying to prove myself…
to no avail.

You see… No one wanted a "throw away girl."
That is how they saw me,
it is what they wanted to believe
after he raped me.

Scholarship thrown out…
all that hard work…
I'd never even been kissed!
A virgin at seventeen.

They tried to kick me out of college
because I wasn't quiet,
because I reported it.
I got to stay, but I should have left.

I was branded,
blacklisted,
scarlet lettered
for wanting justice.

I wonder how different my life would've been?
I wonder if I could've gone on to Broadway,

if it had never happened,
if I had stayed home for a year?

If I had kept my mouth shut?
All it did was hurt ME to tell.
My reputation, my career,
my parents' pockets.

I went from goody two-shoes
to the girl everyone claimed I was...
What was the point
if I was going to be punished anyway?

He got off scot-free.
They kicked him out
but no time served,
no apology...

Three others came forward.
They were virgins too!
It didn't matter,
the school brushed it under the rug.

"Boys will be boys!"
That's what they said.
"You should've been more careful."
"You shouldn't have been alone with him."

It was MY FAULT?!
WHAT?!
My parents were never as close after that.
I was never the same.

I've spent my entire life trying to get my dignity back.
Trying to forgive that girl who I learned to blame.
"I should've stayed in."
"I should've been more careful."

NO!
HE SHOULD'VE BEEN ARRESTED!
HE SHOULD'VE BEEN PUNISHED!
HE SHOULD'VE KEPT HIS HANDS TO HIMSELF!
HE SHOULD'VE HAD TO PAY!
HE OWES ME AN APOLOGY!
HE OWES THE OTHERS AN APOLOGY!
HE DESERVED TO BE CASTRATED!
HE DESERVES TO ROT IN HELL!

Church tells me that again,
it's my turn…
I am the one that has to forgive
with no apology?

I thought I had,
I've tried…
But if I found out he died…
I would travel to spit on his grave

Brandy Lane

D. RODGERS

HOPELESS CAUSE

I am tired of being alone
And sick of feeling the pain.
When will it go away?
Does it ever leave?
Life is too overwhelming.
And absolutely unbearable.
I don't want to do this anymore
Because I can't keep going.
My heart cries out day and night
With no relief.
What is the point of carrying on?
Where will it get me?
Nowhere.
Who will miss me when I am gone?
Only my children,
And not even all of them.
I want to piece my heart back together and can't.
There are too many shards.
I am just a lost cause.
Who will love me for me,
If I can't even love myself?
And the healing process seems to be dragging on...
Just when I feel like I have somewhat of a handle on it,
Something triggers me.

I feel my world come crashing down all around me
And it seems I haven't gotten anywhere.
Then,
I am gently reminded by a dear friend
That I am doing just fine
And that I have come a long way...
Sure doesn't feel like it on days like today.
I try to keep my mind on positive things.
Then,
Anxiety comes along
With best friend depression
And pulls the rug out from under me.
Desperately,
I sweep all the shattered pieces of my heart
Back under that proverbial rug,
Hoping no one will notice
I am a hopeless cause...
Does anyone ever notice?
Does anyone even care?
What's the point of life
If it leaves me feeling helpless
Hopeless
And useless...

D. Rodgers

THE DARKNESS

The darkness…
The darkness is closing in on me
I can't…
I can't breathe
I can't see
I can't feel.
My hope…
My hope is gone.
Why?
What is the point of this life?
Why do I continue to have seemingly loving
And caring people come into my life
Only to leave?
Am I really that bad of a person
That no one wants me around?
I guess I am.
I don't want to be here anymore
Than anyone else wants me to be.
Throughout my life,
All I have ever known is rejection.
I am finished with this life.
I am finished living.
If you see me tomorrow,
Will you stay?

D. Rodgers

KELLI J GAVIN

NOT REALLY SURE

I am not really sure what happened last night.
I woke this morning to find my middle finger sliced as if I had been in a bar fight.
Who was I fighting?
Or was I the one assaulting another?
The bottoms of my feet are indented with pebble marks and scratched as if sticks and branches were all along my chosen path.
Who was I running from?
Or was it I that was doing the chasing?
My feet are calloused, and the skin is falling off in sheets.
Barefoot, my travels didn't take me very far.
I woke confused in the same bed where the night before I attempted to rest my weary head.
Even when I believed my mind was finally giving me a break and falling into the land of not remembering.
My body again has betrayed me.
My legs must have been working hard to keep up, as every muscle aches.
My arms feel weakened, as if crawling was the only means of transportation.

What was I after?

What did I desire so desperately?

As Darkness Falls

Everything I did last night was for naught.
Every part of my body is paying the price for whatever happened, all
while I thought I was sleeping.
Sleep now doesn't seem to be a precious commodity when it comes
time to face it tonight.
Almost dreaded, I may avoid it a bit longer.
My body can't take much more of this.

Kelli J Gavin

CONSTRICTION

It hurts more every day
The tightness
The grasp
The hold
Wondering when it will end
If it will end
The tears are constant
I can't seem to wipe them
They keep reappearing
Falling
Burning
Aching
I've reached my limit
Don't believe I can continue
Immobilized by pain
Held captive by the weight
Fearful this is all I am
My chest is constricted
Can't take a full breath
Now is when I cave
Implode
Fade away
I have nothing left to give
Never anything to offer
All strength depleted
Yet I will not stop
Searching

As Darkness Falls

Wishing
Hoping
There has to be more
Something's gotta give
Release the pressure
The tightness
The constant hold
It must stop
Falling
Burning
Aching
This constriction must cease

Kelli J Gavin

SA QUINOX

PAST LIFETIMES REVERBERATE

Today feels strangely familiar.
As if reaped from pedestrian ashes,
or stolen from ancient homes.

Today floats between silver linings, breathes heavy,
and flows liquescent from rusted mugs.
I slip these wounded hands
into centuries of forgotten agony
carved by bloody nails
into even bloodier walls.
I find myself down on my knees,
weeping from different eyes;
echoing from sacred burial grounds.
I have woken up inside a different time,
to set my eyes on the cold shade
of a younger moon,
to feel, to break, and to mourn
all over again.

SA Quinox

CALL ME

Call me
when the soul wanders
and madness throbs angrily
inside dazed throats.

Call me
when your lifeblood
grinds down weary spines,
carving barbed tunnels
into restless hearts.
When you no longer
recognise the hymn
that ties your feet
to this world.

Call me
when you feel forsaken
and your eyes grow weary
and you no longer see
a light behind sacred doors.

Call me
when peace eludes you,
yet you ache to find
nothing else.
Let us walk together

through peripheral gates.
Into hidden chambers

that keep our names
enshrined on their walls.
Like an entombment of our sorrow.
Like a rite to lay our souls
to solemn rest.

SA Quinox

A WORLD WITHOUT TIME

I wanted to fly,
to tear my feet
from this earth
and not come down
before this wintry hue
dripped from my bones.

I wanted to run
and fold my tongue
into wicked angles
before speaking
of the anguish that
held me down.

I ached to crawl
away from a
most inviting ending
and keep my palms
from oozing
on those that
would not see me
stitched back up

even if I'd pleaded
for my life.

I had to untie
my soul from
pasts that dripped

like pastel melancholy
from my lips.

Time froze willingly
on this centuries-old spine.
There no longer was
a loop of hurt
inside this world.

It stopped moving.
It stopped dancing.
It stopped spinning.

My knees no longer
knew of yearning.
My feet no longer
capable of running.

I spent this lifetime
holed inside the abyss.
Nothing stared back,
nothing but my own
life deflated eyes.
Nothing.
Nothing.

There is nothing
inside this world
deprived of time.

SA Quinox

PT MULDOON

THE BATTLE

You say that you can beat this
Tell yourself that you're all in
So you pull into your riggin
Cause the ride's set to begin
The meds will tear you sideways
Good friends will see you sick
You'll fight for things you once had
Climb that steep hill brick by brick
The poisons you ingest to fight
Will exact their heavy cost
Some days to count the victories
While many others pain and loss
You'll see good friends surrender
And their pain will cut you deep
As each new morning's sunrise
Shows new scars for you to keep
This monster is well-mounted
And if you let him gain he'll ride
He fights with every tool he has
From his place down deep inside
There ain't no finish buzzers
Ain't no rescue pick-up men
As each ride slows just a little
Soon the next one starts again

You'll find a little courage grow
Then maybe catch a tiny break
Start to think you're finally fading
When you've had all you can take
There ain't no cure for this one
Just great endless epic fight
As you struggle to stay seated
On this ride to reach warm light
So if you see me getting angry
When the darkness pulls me in
If I go where you cant find me
Know I'll ride back out again

I won't quit when it gets scary
I signed on to see this through
The monster's in there waiting
So I have fighting left to do

PT Muldoon

AN UNMADE BED

Upon this ragged bed of life
Where time just plays on thru
Far beyond that bitter edge
Out where our dreams undo
There hides within a sanctity
Deep inside that searing pain
Where the bitter poison swims
Into that worn but willing vein
As the monster lurks inside
And he waits another chance
To finally remove fate's mask
And then engage our dance
There are hard adversaries
That we all must face alone
We rail against their darkness
Until our own lights shone
For us to truly live and dream
We all must face the fact
That all of life in time will end
And one day play the final act
Deep in that darkened corner
Where the gravely injured bled
Remain the dreams unfinished
Left in an unmade bed

PT Muldoon

THE VOYAGE

It's the voyage of the fiercest
Brave warriors on their quest
To work with what's remaining
As they seek to find their best
Perhaps to never overcome
But they are willing to still try
They don the capes of heroes
As they boldly charge that sky
A mother with a little child
Wig replacing her lost hair
She lost in heat of battle
That cancer still in there
Soldier who returned from war
With spine too broke to mend
He straps into a chair of wheels
Then he joins that fight again
When I was young and willing
I admired those who played
All my idols are now different
The few who fought and stayed
Capes they wear are ragged
From wars too tough to fight
But they are my new heroes
As they soar high into the light
And maybe just one moment
Is all that's left for them to win
This battle knocks them over

As Darkness Falls

Yet they rise back up again
And in the silence of the night
Their capes get scarred and torn
But they wear em still with honor
The brave heroes tired and worn
Somewhere past the shadows
Another warrior joins this fray
Pulls on their cape of heroes
Then fights just one more day

PT Muldoon

ASHLEY NICOLSON

SELFLESS

"Just be yourself" echoes through my mind in increasing volumes
Which self do they mean?
Which me do you want today?
I cycle through a maddening menagerie of different minds and motifs
My swirling and swaying is not like it's portrayed in the books and
movies
This insanity is not beautiful
This darkness is not harrowing
These memories swirling with a near BB style laziness yet hitting my
almost bulletproof soul with a force resembling an AK47
Chipping away at my stoic silence as my heart bellows for release
One day all of my selves will meet
The brave facade will crumble
And a thousand me's will crumble
Laying shattered at your feet

Ashley Nicolson

STARDUST

Every time I walk by a mirror now, I avert my gaze.
Unwilling to make eye contact with this monstrosity I've become.
You planted entire galaxies in my soul.
They used to shine through at the slightest glance.
In your heartbreaking absence, I have let the brightest of our stars go
supernova.
I fear the nothingness lingering behind my own gaze.
Undoubtedly, I will be annihilated by what lingers within the deepest
parts of me.
The places within myself that you curated to hold the mended you
made.
The broken that I was, into the shattered I am now.
I barely recall the in-between.
The brilliance of hundreds of thousands of pieces of my very own
stardust that you expertly crafted into a new beautiful.
It left with you.
Perhaps to carry you to the stars.
Surely I had to become nothing but this black hole in order for you to
find your way home.

Ashley Nicolson

JERILYN SCAVO REED

NO STRANGER

I am especially drawn to the darkest places within you.
I notice each and every injury, whether it is a festering wound or a
tiny scratch.
Those places within you are where you hold your fury;
You can't hide from me.
I can smell it.
I can taste it.
I know pain, and I know you,
I know the darkness
It knows me too,
It's all around us.
Scream as loud as you need
Our demons and I don't mind.

Jerilyn Scavo Reed

BRENDA CIERNIAK

ENDLESS FIRE

I drag myself out of the darkness as some kind of sanity returns,
had to force my grief down deep inside, try to lessen how it burns.
Gotta damp that fire down some, so I can live through all my days;
but don't be fooled by appearances because it never goes away.
I can't let it fully rage and burn, sit and wallow in my pain;
I know that I can't live that way, always dancing in it's flame.
Since the day you died there's been a hole,
a wound that just won't heal,
like part of me is forever missing, a loss I'll always feel.
So I push it down to a deep dark place,
although some flames still break through.
Sometimes a random sound, a smell,
instantly brings me thoughts of you,
then the pain hits like a hand grenade and explodes inside my heart.
I feel like I can't catch my breath as my soul is torn apart.
I hurt, I cry, push it down again, and try to go about my day,
how else could I continue living, I don't know of any other way.
Because to give my life up willingly,
when you got no choice to live or not,
would be a dishonour to your memory,
by wasting the life that I've got.

Brenda Cierniak

THE PIT

At the bottom of a deep dark pit, trying to find the strength to climb,
dark shadows try and reach for me, a familiar paradigm.
I climb a little every day, my ascent painful and slow,
not sure if I can reach the top, but the darkness waits below.
I know if I stop moving, the dark will suffocate my soul,
and maybe I'll be overwhelmed as the shadows take their toll.
So I claw and grasp at what I can as I climb towards the top,
so tired and bone-weary but knowing I can never stop.

Brenda Cierniak

VALERIE MESTA

DYING MONSTER

I am the therapy that finds the blood in your ash-stricken heart and bleeds it.

I'm the blackening of your cold dead skin and the stillness of your freezing fear.
I am the pain of your death while you live and the paranoia that begs for an early end.

You once thought I was sweet and weak...
But now you see that I have been killing you since your first sin.
My voice is that of a siren, gracefully spilling your painful truths.
You're a fucken monster, and now everyone knows it.

You're the victim now...

How does it feel to know you're to die alone with people too disgusted to mourn your death?

Everything set before you is a trick.
You will never have happiness long enough to even know it exists.

You're just a fucken monster pretending to be human.

A fucken monster being tortured since your very first sin.

You're a fucken monster, and I will scream your fucken dirty secrets.

You're no longer creeping...
You're hiding now.

Monsters have nightmares too...

There's nothing more horrifying to a monster than the truth.

You're a fucken disgusting monster, and now everyone knows it.

Valerie Mesta

ONLY TIME RELIEVES

When your heart breaks, it fucken breaks.

There's no explaining the reason or putting your heart at ease any sooner than it's ready.

I've cried a million times from that deep pain that demands liquid salt...

There's no rushing the process.
It's one day at a time.
It's walking around with a knife in your chest…
It's fucken messy with wounds bleeding and lumps in your throat.
I've been there, and that darkness still comes knocking.
It's over, but it really isn't.
It's bittersweet.

Take me to the trees.

Valerie Mesta

OFFENDERS BEWARE

Normal has no home with me.
Rage is a wonderful mess.
Shake my hand...

Bend around my mind.
Bend all you can.
Sick is what I am.
Contagious is what I'm not, but you will flee all the same.
Satisfaction to my day.
Stay away so I don't have to try to explain.
Stay away...

PTSD, and a sprinkle of Rage...

Bipolar me will tarnish your day.
You will never understand my fears.
You will never understand the me that isn't me...

The desolate creation of Molestation, Physical Abuse, Verbal abuse, and Rape!
Paint me Not a Victim for you are mine!
I'm ice cold and brilliant in my revenge.
I am easy on the eyes...

I'm a wonderful disguise!
I'll fight with my word's, even though I can't sleep.
You will be the victim of you!
Karma and God will find you!
But first you will see me.
The other me...

As Darkness Falls

Such things that consume my mind...

What you have done to me is nothing compared to my friend
Beelzebub!
My mind's damaged Razor Sharp.
The Blood my mind spills is Beautiful, and warm like Family.
I'm the creature that feeds off the stench of your decomposing corps.
In my mind all that's gory is miraculous art.
You are Glorious in your Death!
And it is ART!
Fantastic ART!
You will be unique in your final pose...

As unique as your Blood on my paint brush.
Victims, Vast!
My gallery is full.
Such Monster's you all are!
But as I write, and create...

I'm the monster Today.
For Survivors of hate I'll create!
No victims of innocence will bleed today.
I have spray paint filled with the blood of the asshole who stole
comfort from your night.
Cry not!
You're composing the nightmares this time!
Set your hurt free...

Let them Bleed.
It's time for art's and craft's...

Carry your monsters to me!

Valerie Mesta

AMY PASZTAS

IN MEMORIAM LJK...

There's mist on the horizon
That shines like broken glass
In amongst the darkness
Of losses that are past.
And ghosts, they may come calling
For ever are they near
And as the darkness lingers
It brings with it some fear
Of loneliness and heartache
Of blood spilled on the ground
Of fences that are broken
And life without the sound
And here without the trappings
No walls to hide behind
In amongst my shadows
And lost inside my mind
I'm dancing with my demons
And learning to be still
For loss will always change us
And break apart our will
And like the glass that's broken
We never are the same
But we are made much stronger
For going through the pain

So if your heart is breaking
Just know you're not alone
For I too have been shattered
I am not made of stone
I stand beneath the storm clouds
And here I am at peace
And with the tears now flowing
I've finally found release.

Amy Pasztas

AVANT AVANT-GARDE

ORPHANED

Strength; I saw.
It was a mantra giving offering of your devotion
The phoenix rising-
A guardian of heart, fanning flames of Protection

Compassion; I saw.
Drops of quench to the thirst of a soul in anguish
My Mother Teresa-
Patron saint of nurture, displaying the unconditional of Acceptance

Decisions; I saw...
Obligation gagged and labored
worth left on a ventilator-
Life after death transferred to predator, you saw husband
Eulogy printed, victim, never saw as daughter...

Avant-Avant-garde

VACANCIES

"I'm homesick..."

A nomad lost without sojourn;
trading voyage for the land of
contentment-

Winds without the strength to create
breeze; suffocating within a funnel.

A Sunrise without power;
no break of horizon for
beaming-

Skies with limits, watching this eclipse
drown sunrise like a black hole.

"I'm homesick..."

A touch with no fingers
to interpret the message;
illiterate, yet having mastered braille-

A voice without embodiment of
vocal cord-
a whisper screaming in a room full of deaf.

This waterfall, damned to no
cascade:
rapids, now just a passionate trickle-

As Darkness Falls

"I'm homesick…"
Said, the mangled keys of my soul,
staring into the locked house
I once called- marriage…

Avant Avant-garde

JAMIE SANTOMASSO

REWIND

I press rewind
And play your memory on repeat
A haunting rerun in my mind
Soft echoes ricochet off reluctant reminders
Of what-ifs and what could-have-beens
The recordings of you left to remind
Memoirs that sound at resounding feat

...I press rewind

Buttons worn clean of markings from constant press
The compulsive need to feel you once more consumes me
Love once had our hearts entwined
Two souls merged into one beat
A haunting rerun in my mind
We were as one...
Lost within each other
Without you I feel blind
I'd give forever to again feel that complete

...I press rewind

Do angels hear wishes?
Do they grant desperate pleas?
Relief... Peace... Solace I'm unable to find...
If only once more our auras could meet

As Darkness Falls

A haunting rerun in my mind
Peace eternally denied
Memories destined to play on repeat

I press rewind...

I press rewind

Jamie Santomasso

THE MEMORY OF YOU

In love's lost memory, I whisper goodbyes
Haunting epitaphs... sweet nothing's eulogy spoken
They remind me of better days
The memory of you still haunts me
Your voice echoes in my mind
A mournful serenade played on repeat
The past revisits my memory through you
I can still feel your touch
Traces of you left on my skin
Mental remnants I can't reprieve myself from
You follow me in my dreams
The memory of you still haunts me
With reluctant resolve, I face mirrored truths
A silent send off for times once held
Your image I keep with me
You will live on forever through my words
I linger over the scrapbook of us
Its pages still bare
But still, I can't ignore the etching you left within me
The memory of you still haunts me
Sweet nothing's eulogy spoken in love's lost memory
I whisper goodbyes
Haunting epitaphs; they remind me of better days

Jamie Santomasso

REDEMPTION OF THE REAVER

To him she handed her heart

"Be gentle" she spoke, " it's held together only by stitches of hope"

"Why this gift?" he asked "I am not deserving of such an offering; my monster knows only how to destroy."

"I do not fear your demons," she replied.

"In you I see redemption, for you are not damned to your self-imposed prison."

He took her endowment and knew her love was pure, wanting only to embrace him. It was his last redemption.

He vowed to protect her; she was his anchor, his lifeline from the sea that seeked to drown his ship.

She was salvation. In her was the chance he had searched for, and the wall encasing his heart began to crack.

He reached to open the gate and welcome her home into his kingdom.

They embraced, and he vowed to her that her journey was no longer alone; they would move ahead side by side.

He took her hand, and they stepped forward.

Bliss surrounded her. She was finally home. As she looked upon him with adoration, she knew her gift was safe.

But in the distance, his dark clouds followed. Their invisible noose still tethered to his neck.

They whispered their song, a trance he could not ignore.

For he was a monster, unable to change.

He pleaded silently: Release me. I have fulfilled my contract. Grant me my freedom.

They would not relinquish him.

With a heavy mind, he studied her gift in his hand, the delicate symbol of her trust and adoration.

Whispering a silent apology, he closed his fist and crushed her heart, the jagged pieces projecting and piercing her skin.

She fell to the ground, agony washing over her. She looked at him and pleaded, desperate to reach him.

But the demon stood in his place, and she realized this had always been his true form. She held herself as sorrow poured from her eyes.

The devastation in her cries cut into him, and he felt her pain flow from her wounds. The gravity of his actions hit him, and he fell to his knees.

He held the broken pieces of her heart as he pleaded for her hand.

"Save me. You are my Beautiful Star, my home. I knew not love until now. I beg for atonement, a chance at redemption."

In silence, she stood. An empty hole resided where her heart once was. Where once she felt love, betrayal now lived.

She met his gaze, but only a vacant stare remained within her.

As Darkness Falls

"Your demon has won," she whispered, defeated. A single tear fell from his eye as she turned her back and stepped away, leaving him alone on the ground.

The monster rose and said his heartbroken goodbye. He bathed in the acceptance of his fate. From the ground he picked up a fragment of her heart, a reminder of his loss.

He yearned for forgiveness, a chance to hold his love one last time.

But he was the demon; this was his prison. His eternal path to walk alone.

He looked back at his broken love one last time then turned to take his ill-fated passage.

Jamie Santomasso

STEPHANIE MUELLER

THE CROW'S CRY

Your gravel voice circles round,
waking me from the dreams in which I drown.
Early each dawn,
the coldness of your CAW-CAW, CAW-CAW
echoes in my ears,
an unwelcome reminder
that his time on Earth is drawing near.
With your sleek, black feathers in flight,
you steal the Sun's life-giving Light.
As you soar, hovering overhead,
you foreshadow the loss of a precious friend.
Even now, as I hold him in my arms,
sleeping ever so comfortably
free from worldly harm,
your cry relentlessly breaks the silence
warning that no existence here is timeless.
Then, without notice, you suddenly arrive,
perched on my back porch step
black as night,
as if to announce his time has come
to let go of the pain,
and follow the Angels' guiding flame.
With one last labored breath,
may he forever find his eternal rest,

As Darkness Falls

may he now divinely rise
and join the stars living beyond the sky.

Stephanie Mueller

WHERE IS THE LOVE TO GO?

When love is not gone,
but too weak to hold on,
do we turn and walk away
or continue to dance the masquerade?

Remember how moonlit strolls and fireflies
kissed our cheeks and graced our skies?
How timeless talks whispered on the breeze
sparking a flame in the tender hearts of two teens?

And somehow twenty years have drifted away,
our once carefree spirits have now turned gray.
Remnants of reality burrowed deep within our souls,
changing us for a lifetime, no longer to be whole.

Yet love still brushes the lips that kiss
reminding us that joyful times did once exist.
Tales of devotion etched high in stardust above
years before our hearts ever met and fell in love.

So, who among us could have foretold
how our future dreams would fall and unfold
to reveal a vision crushing and unforeseen
as infertility wedged its savage fangs in between?

The shiver of December has now come to stay
upon a marriage never thought to fail or fray.
Even though the ember of love still burns within,
is the flame strong enough for grace to win?

As Darkness Falls

Or have the hands of darkness stretched too far,
their roots of silence carved too deep a scar?
For now, in two separate houses do we sleep
while the hallways cry out in guilt and grief.

If the flame of love once ignited never dies,
do we carry on despite the hurt in our eyes?
And if so, then where is the love to go
when our branches must part in order to grow?

Unsure of our wings, we must learn to fly,
yet how do we leap forward without saying goodbye?
When our hearts are bound by an invisible thread
will our journey as one now come to an end?

I fear the answers dwell in a plan yet to be told,
not until looking back will the reason truly be known...
Why our journey as one
was destined to become
a story of two souls forever bound,
whose paths were fated to walk separate ground.

Stephanie Mueller

C.N. GREER

SO MUCH

There was so much I wanted to say to you.
I had it all planned out.
The stories I wanted to tell,
the memories we would share.
But now that I'm here, I can't find the words.
You've never felt more distant, and
our reality has never felt more real.
So, I say nothing. And the minutes pass.
I don't feel you anymore, and that scares me
more than anything else in this world.
I'm afraid to let you go. I'm afraid that I'll forget,
even though you're so much a part of me
that losing you is like losing myself.
And there's nothing either of us can do to stop it.
This isn't what I wanted for you.
This isn't how I thought it would end.
But even I can't fight death.
So instead, I place a kiss upon your stone,
and I wipe my tears as I walk away.

C.N. Greer

SMILE AT THE SHORELINE

I'm a stranger to Sleep, an acquaintance to Nightmare.
My sanctuary's left me for a land dark and bare.

Struggling for light, sweet relief's yet to come.
I still know the ache, but I only feel numb.

It's a silent emptiness that's consuming my soul.
My life continues as before, but I have yet to feel whole.

I'm a shadow on the outside looking into my world.
I'm not quite connected to the tears of the girl.

You've stolen my heart; you've stolen my life force.
Now I'm left to stumble down this uneven course.

You pushed, and you prodded, using guilt as your pole.
You kept breaking my strength, leaving in your wake gaping holes.

You need to feel guilty. You deserve the heavy load.
Now you can feel what I've felt struggling down rocky roads.

Carry that burden while fighting alone in the dark.
Then you'll know how I felt while you were breaking my heart.

Feel the bite of the ache, the sting of the hurt.
Feel the pain press upon you as the hellfire burns.

My mind's chained to you, held fast, not unlocked.
Your heart holds the key, but that path I've blocked.

It's a terrifying prison, for I long to be free.
I only fear if you come close, you'll end up chained to me.

So, I carry these irons through the dark waters near shore,
The shackles that bind me to the pain on the floor.

Do you feel how I feel? Have you caught a glimpse of it yet?
Have you felt the yearning, seen the light you can't get?

Have you crashed through the ocean unable to breathe?
I don't reach for you. I'm reaching for me.

You are the black waters, the guilt, and shame crashing down.
As the sharp sorrow surrounds me, you take my breath. I start to drown.

But though I'm thrashed by the waves, I'll reach the surface yet.
Though I may be pummeled by waters, my strength you won't get.

I'll live again, breathe in the pain. I'll smile stronger than before.
And while your memory may haunt me, I'm standing solid on the shore.

C.N. Greer

SHARP OBJECTS

You held the knife against your skin
and wondered why you didn't bleed.
Why, when you pressed your hand
upon the blade,
it was my palm that ran with red.
So, you cut deeper.
You dug the edge in so forcefully
you could see the bone.
Still, you felt nothing.
But you heard the scream.
You saw my tears.
You knew it was my throat that
was raw with pain,
my flesh you were tearing to shreds.
So, you ran the blade across my wrists,
wondering if you would feel me, too.
"I don't understand," you told me.
"Why do you bleed when I hurt,
But I feel nothing when I cut you?"
"This is what being loved by me looks like,"
I replied, our life's blood pouring over my hands.
"People really shouldn't give me sharp objects."

C.N. Greer

B. VIGIL

BEAUTY IN DARKNESS

She was the beauty of darkness,
the queen of the moonlight,
the beacon for all of the lost souls.
She survived all of the fires
that were meant to destroy her,
but she was swallowed by the darkness whole.
She was an angel with black wings,
followed by all pretty dark things,
showing us the beauty in it all.
She blazed the path for the brokenhearted,
made you forget where you started,
she became the stars that you follow
when darkness falls.
Her black heart is still beating,
Still shining and bleeding,
Still standing despite it all.

B. Vigil

AS THE DARKNESS FALLS

The vastness of the darkness captivated the lost souls who were stuck in it for so long.
Making friends out of monsters because our souls know they just want to belong.
We thrive in the twilight and fall in love with the moonlight, answering when the wolves call.
Like a lotus flower, growing in the dark muddy waters; Blooming despite it all.
We love in the shadows and dance when the gods fight; as the darkness falls.

B. Vigil

SHAWNA OLIBAMOYO

TIME WILL TELL

Time will tell
It always seems
That when in need
There is no seed
Waiting to be
Free to feel again
Alive to inspire
In faded desire
Somehow all tangled
In a web of emotion
To break through
Not a slight notion
The heart that beats
Alone and tattered
Tempted to open up
Too afraid too shattered
Lost in the shuffle
Wanting to be found
Searching and searching
But no one is around
Wondrous dreams
That give some hope
Floating through reality
Finding a way to cope

As Darkness Falls

Perhaps there is
The truth of bliss
For now is without
Looked over another miss
The sun keeps rising
Whether or not its seen
Shinning and so bold
Always warm never cold
Time will tell
It always seems
That maybe one day
I can live my dreams

Shawna Olibamoyo

NOWHERE

In the middle of nowhere
Looking for the sun
Only finding dark clouds
That I can not reach
Searching for answers
Some reason for the chaos
Of life's uncertainty
Distant illusions of love
That float like balloons
Taunting my heart
Unaware
Of the seamless scraps
They leave behind
Tossed aside
On a broken road
To nowhere
I find myself
Alone

Shawna Olibamoyo

SHARIL MILLER

LONE WOLF

You were born to sit behind the wheel and drive
It's what kept your wandering spirit alive
You were a lone wolf, although you sometimes traveled in packs
Always knowing you had each other's backs
A bunk for your bed and truck stop eats definitely were not frills
But the life you so loved always paid the bills
Driving all those miles in your truck
Always meant more to you than just making a buck
Over those highways, you were known as Gravytrain
Earning membership into The Million Mile Club was one of your
claims to fame
In another life, you must have been a gypsy
You loved the long hauls wandering cross-country
Miles away, you would roam
But, I always knew you would come home
There was only one trip I was not ready for you to make
When you left this world causing my heart to break
So much of you is left behind
You are never far from my mind
As I wipe tears away from my eyes
I smile knowing you are driving your big rig in the skies

Sharil Miller

ASTRAY

When I first met you, I was 22 months old
Your entrance into this world was nothing less than bold

You arrived in the world a little too early
Causing everyone around us a lot of worry

When you were strong enough, you came home to live with us
Family and friends all made quite a fuss
Growing up we were always best friends and partners in crime
Our antics and adventures were some of our best times

Your best friend became mine too
And it wasn't long before you were cringing about wearing a tuxedo
of baby blue

At our wedding, you stood beside us as our best man
You always were our biggest fan

At some point, life broke you down
Dulling the mischievous glimmer in your eyes of brown

I knew you fought many demons in life
But no one fully understood your struggles and strife

You chose to leave us one January night
Our shock and dismay, we had to fight

When I saw you lying on the table in that gown
I saw a smile on your face where I thought would be a frown

At that moment, you were finally at rest
While my bittersweet tears fell freely upon your still chest

As Darkness Falls

That's when I knew you were at peace
Because in your heart what you needed was that final release

Some may say suicide is a coward's way
But sadly, your broken spirit just got lost and simply went astray

Sharil Miller

ALWAYS MY HERO

I was your hero... it's what you always said
But truth be told, you were always my hero instead
As much as you were torn between this world and the next, I wanted you to know
I was just as torn for wanting you to stay, but it was ok for you to go
While you were standing with one foot in each world deciding to choose
I was standing right there by your side in the middle of a memory with you
Within a fleeting moment the wings of your soul took you to a place for you to be free
In my heart, I know you're still here by my side, but you seem so very far away from me
You were there for my first breath, and I was there for your last
Although we had many years together, the time moved way too fast
With tears flowing freely and my love pouring deeply beside your lifeless body I knelt
My hero was gone right before my eyes... lost and alone to the very depth of my core I felt
When your soul took flight that heartbreaking night, with it flew my sense of identity
To find myself I'll do my best to honor your life and to become the hero you believed me to be

Sharil Miller

BIANCA MARIE NERY

HAPPY AGAIN

Can you see
past the painted-on smile
I keep wearing
to scare away
the well-wishers
and pitiful gazes
raining down on me?

My glass house
is full of curtains
to keep the sun
from shining through.

Please
just let me
stay in the dark
a little longer.
I promise
to come out
once the noise
inside my head
finally dies down.

I swear
I will be
happy again

in time.
But for now
just let me be
lonely
one more time.

Bianca Marie Nery

THE EVOLUTION OF MY ROMANTIC ENDEAVOR

I.

I wore your presence
like a sweater,
if only to keep out the cold
that came when you walked into my life.

II.

I trod lightly
on your scars,
listened
to your heart,
burned myself
with your flame,
and let all of it
consume me,
and feed me,
and take me,
and make me
your own.

III.

Waking up
was falling down
from a high I never knew I've reached.

As Darkness Falls

Where would I be now
if I had never
found my feet
and used them
to walk away
from you?

Bianca Marie Nery

MARGIE WATTS

HAPPY ENDINGS

There are no Happy Endings here in the darkness.

Fairytales nor love exist. There is nothing but pain here. Sadistic pain. Memories circling around in your mind. While twisted, dirty secrets kept with the ugliness endured are locked away from the light. Forgotten memories but remembered. Until finally, you can bear it no longer; then the howls of agony ring through the air as rivers of tears flow. Finally, the sound of a breaking heart as the soul begs for mercy.

Darkness.

There are no Happy Endings in the darkness.

Margie Watts

MESSAGES

I listened to your messages today. I don't know why really. I woke up and felt a deep heaviness around my heart. I had been deleting prior messages without listening to them when you called. Finally, I blocked your number so I wouldn't know you were calling. Your messages were going straight to voicemail, and that was that. But even your blocked messages were there. So as tears began to flow, I decided to listen to them. There were only four.

"Call me, please."

"Are you going to call me back?"

"Please call me, I love you."

"Please, please call me."

As I listened to each one, I could hear the desperation and the sadness in your voice. Then, the sound of brokenness. I had heard those same words before, the same sounds of sadness and desperation and finally brokenness. That had been me at one time. So many times that had been me. As I gathered myself, I called you. I still can't explain why. What was I going to say when you answered? Seven, eight rings, no answer. I took it as a sign as I hung up; We were meant not to speak to each other.

Wiping my tears, I decided as I deleted the messages one by one, it was time, time to close the book of us. However, my heart knew it would not remain that way forever.

Margie Watts

WILL HOEYE

LOVE IS A SIN

Love is a sin.
How can it be anything but?
Bliss at first,
But losing it seems a must.
Torn and battered,
Self medication.
Life nearing tatters.
Try to reach for you,
But still so afraid.
Coming unglued,
Heart becoming frayed.
Tired of being alone,
But don't want to talk.
Accepting you're gone,
Drinking till I can't walk.
Hoping this weight will lift,
Knowing it won't.
Mind constantly adrift,
It's still you I want.
Needing a distraction,
Wanting more than a night.
More than basic satisfaction,
Something worth the fight.
But what would be the point?

When does the struggle end?
This heart need not be joined,
Because, after all, Love is a Sin.

Will Hoeye

SWEET POISON

The well is deep
I dug it myself
A dark little place
Where my soul can weep
A place to hide
Just for awhile
Unburden my mind
So that I can smile
Sometimes I get stuck
That poison of doubt
Tastes so sweet
But I make it through
By sheer force
And claw my way out
A little time is all I need
A few hours to allow
My heart to bleed
Purge the pain
Let it all go
Then I can raise my head
Fake a smile
And still live…
in pretend

Will Hoeye

WOUNDED

Wounds reopened,
Scars torn apart,
Suffering surfaces,
Yet I refuse to close my heart.
The honeymoon was bliss,
The pain gorgeous.
Only sand can erase,
That heavenly kiss.
The memories brought to view,
By nothing more than a whisper
Of a song, reminding me of you.
Just for a moment,
I relive that dream.
Refusing to wake,
Fearing my own scream.
Yes, my heart still aches.
Yes, my mind still shakes.
But, I wouldn't dare forget that time.
That drop of life, when you were mine.
I cherish those beautiful days,
Few they may be.
Without them, I would've never known
That second of love, over which I still moan.

Will Hoeye

ANN MARIE ELEAZER

WEEPING WILD ORCHIDS

I locked fingers and embraced the icy depths of grief many a time, but nothing could prepare me for the freshly dug grave that trembled within my heart's chamber the day I finally said goodbye.

Death's look-alike peeked around every corner and danced upon those unexpected gasps for breath, staring me down like a well-polished gravestone as I remembered every chance I gave you and every moment in weeping despair.

And while my soul crooned a sigh of relief and my mind wept in standing ovation, my heart buried a piece of herself knowing that one day, her wild orchids would bloom again.

Ann Marie Eleazer

GYPSY'S REVERIE

WAITING IN DARKNESS

Many are afraid of the dark, fearing the monsters creeping there,
Concealed in the closet, or hiding under the bed.
I lie awake at night also, although I know it isn't monsters that I fear.
It is the Truth that escapes at night:
The thoughts that I avoid so conveniently during daytime,
sweeping them under the bed and trapping them in closets,
emerge with the darkness.
When the sun goes down and sleep eludes me,
Truth breaks the locks of denial I have bound it with
and confronts me once again.
Am I really happy?
Am I living the life I should be?
Do I like who I've become?
Is this all there is???
In the daylight, I can go through life, insisting that I'm fine...
but I dread the coming of the dark--
For I know the Truth that lurks there,
Lying in wait...It is coming for me.

Gypsy's Reverie

NIGHTLY ROUTINE

Another day of neglect led to another night of anguish;
Desolation of dashed hopes that perhaps this day would be
different...
Though in the depths of her soul she knew that change wouldn't
come.
The truth was that her husband existed in name only, had abandoned
connection with her long ago.
She was forced to live with the constant reminder of his apathy as he
was always just down the hall, just in his own world, just out of
reach.
And so the sun of another day sank along with her spirit, and she
resumed her nightly routine, entering the sanctuary of the shower
where she would surely come undone.
The water merged with her tears, cleansing her soul as she cried out
for absolution from sins that were never hers to begin with...
Begging for tomorrow to be better than today,
Pleading for the strength, hope, and love to make her stay.
As the waters from within joined the downpour around her, she sat
sobbing until she had no tears left to cry.
She stood and dried herself off, trying to erase all evidence of her
agony.
Gazing at the moon which had risen during her torrent of sorrow,
She crawled into bed alone again, bleak hopes for tomorrow.

Gypsy's Reverie

HOMESICK

They say home is where the heart is...
But what if your heart belongs to another?
I gave mine to a man long ago;
Our paths have been divided from the start.
Each time we part, my heart is ripped anew from my chest.
It remains with him as we go our separate ways,
Returning back to the lives we must lead.
There are many miles between him and myself;
Reunions uncertain with weeks in between,
Time and distance cruelly enforcing unwanted separation.
Circumstances creating a daily existence of suffering:
Loneliness at once familiar, and yet,
Also a pain more elusive to identify.
To say that I miss him is a trivialization,
An incomplete assessment of this misery.
Yearning intensifies with each passing day;
The ache takes the breath from my lungs.
I feel displaced and distraught without him near me.
Bereft of belonging, searching for sanctuary...
As the pain of absence heightens, the agony is clarified.
Tears streaming down my face as realization dawns:
I'm homesick for the man who holds my heart with his own.

Gypsy's Reverie

MARY O'CONNELL LOTERBAUER

CAPTIVE SCARS

The scars are my reminder.
The cost of loving too hard.
Or not hard enough
Of speaking when I should have been silent
Or silent when my voice was commanded
The scars are my reminder
That in your eyes I was never enough
That i sold my soul for what I thought was love
And in the end, it was not love at all
But captivity

Mary O'Connell Loterbauer

THE SHIP

Into the darkness I drift
My bed, my blanket, my ship
The waters calm, my mind at rest
Tranquility as I drift

But a pirate boards my vessel
And steals my rest, my sleep
His hands touch my private parts
My soul is shattered deep

My mind escapes to a lifeboat
And I row away for a time
To a place of warmth and protection
Safety if only in my mind

I return to my looted ship
And the asses the loss and carnage
No lifeboat can take me far enough
I am forever damaged

Mary O'Connell Loterbauer

BONDAGE SOUL

I'll never be enough for some.
Ill always be my demons.
No matter how much I transform.
To them there's no redeeming.

To numb was my condition.
To be sober is my choice.
To feel everything at once now,
But not to have a voice

I want to scream to them I'm worth it
To view me as I am today.
To release my soul from bondage.
And send my tears away.

Mary O'Connell Loterbauer

SHARMANI T. ADDERLY

ALIEN

I don't know how to act when I'm with you
Apart I always miss you,
But strangers face to face
Even though I can still feel you

In you I thought I found a home
But sitting cold and alone
Staring at my phone
Waiting on just a message from you
Like being put on the streets
I'm more homeless
Even when I'm with you

An alien try'na act human
Can't last too long
I don't get the jokes
And you don't get mine
Our worlds so far apart
Planets in different galaxies
To co-exist we must redesign

Grinning ear to ear

The happiness was bliss
Now tears roll
Sobbing, no laughter

As Darkness Falls

Those nights we sat and laughed
Under the stars
Are the people that I miss

You don't hear me out
Dismissed, your voice booms
Over mine
Communication one-sided
I just wanted happiness
Not the complicated mess
That erupts over nothing

A life I had before
You walked in and filled my world
Was
Composed and certain
Now
Second-guessing thinking deeply
Before speaking
Better yet no words at all
And still I seem to upset you
Calling unwarranted attention to myself

This is no way to begin the walk we wanted
I have a mind
A heart
A soul
A voice
I stand before you the woman
It took me a long time to be
Regrets behind me

I only asked that you accepted me
As I accepted you
Because my heart would burst
At the sound
Of the words you used to comfort me
The honey you trailed
You trail me to you `
The warmth you promised
The protection you guaranteed

But now…
I don't know how to act when I'm with you
Anxiety replaces excitement
I don't know what lingers in your mind
And instead of love and comfort
Distrust and uncertainty from you
Is what I find

Sharmani T. Adderley

INADEQUATE

It could've been you
But my love
Wasn't enough

My words that
I poured
From the sincerest
Unused regions of my heart
Were inadequate
They weren't enough

My every thought and action
That had you in mind
That made me think
And consider
Your feelings before
My own
Were inadequate
I didn't act
Enough

My decision to see you
Past the epidermis
And pulp
And flesh
To the beautiful flawed soul
You possessed
Was inadequate
Just not enough

The joy you infused me with
The strength you intoxicated me with
The peace you encompassed me with
That stripped away the tattered twines
Of mistrust and skepticism
And instead adorned me
In breathless jeweled tones
That I thought were evident
That you would take great notice of
Was not enough to make you see
The grand effect you had on me

It could've been you
That I gave my whole
Entire heart to
The purest unblemished
Parts of me
The realest uncostumed
Pieces of me
But alas,
All you saw was inadequacy
Just not enough

Sharmani T. Adderley

HUNTED

Shadows follow close behind
Whispers echo in darkened corners
The inevitable I know inevitably
The darkness is angry
And it's coming to get me

Sharmani T. Adderley

JAI K

BACKSTAGE AT A FUNERAL

Death surrounds me as it finds its way inside.
It crawls closer and digs deeper
as it preys on my every fear of outliving it all.
A million grains of earth
cave in on those last breaths.
I'm helpless,
against science, against control,
against the future of a life left
only by locks of hair and photo albums.
Dusted years thrown away.
Handwritten letters and family recipes
quickly read and tossed aside.
There are too many stones to set in place
to stop and find time to remember life.

Jai K

SELF-INFLICTED WOUNDS

The heart bleeds dry through the eyes
and becomes silent when it is truly broken,
not cracked or pierced,
but deeply ripped in half,
every thread sharply cut clean
like all ties with the outside world
the moment the umbilical cord is severed
and you realize it is all up to you to survive.
I picked a fight with my reflection
and let it kick my ass just to feel something.
Shattered glass,
a body cut and bruised,
and while the blood is dry
and it appears that I am healing,
the discoloration shows I'm injured.
I collect scars
like a child who screams bloody murder
from a skinned knee,
and now I cry for nobody.
All words are empty and unnecessary.
Tired of the counterfeit.
No mind kept.
No love lost.
I empty the crypt to make room for myself
at all costs.

Jai K

CHEAP WORDS

Pure silence, and I still can't hear myself think.
I still hear her voice through all the others
talking so loudly.
"My heart breaks for you," they will say,
as if one heart isn't enough.
Thoughts and prayers,
such cheap words,
when there isn't even enough money on earth
to buy the right ones.
Nine hours ridden in silence.
A drive to our bad news,
back to the home of my birth
and my destruction,
as if I already knew.
"Mom didn't make it."
Today is the saddest day.
Let us pray.
And on the day after,
do I want her burned or stuck in a box?
The costs, the urns, the coffins, the signatures,
the lack of final written words.
It's time to start thinking about selling things again,
cleaning out.
The tears don't stop
and twenty minutes of sleep
doesn't help the past forty-eight hours,
while waking up every morning

becomes the real nightmare.
The first time in life where music doesn't help
and being strong is the last thing I want to do.
And then the next day comes
and I finally got some sleep.
Wake up, break down.
A moment alone, break down.
They all arrive to eat.

The jewelry is the first to go through,
what used to be the women's favorite pastime,
but not this time.
Her necklaces and bracelets,
her favorite rings,
the wedding set, her mother's ring
with all of our birthstones,
the trinkets saved since birth,
every piece we ever gave her.
We all break.
And then we all begin again.
Then more news,
more questions,
answers that we don't have.
I was supposed to save her.
She was supposed to help her.
And then in August
you start thinking about Christmas
and how you just might not decorate this year,
and the plants bring a little beauty

to the devastated room,
or at least the needed oxygen
through all the cigarette smoke.
" I'm sorry. Where are my manners?
Did you want some tea?"
I ask while trying to keep busy
and ignore all the questions
people keep wanting to ask me.
"I started the list, but I don't know where it is,
in mom's notebook on the table
but I might've lost the pen.
Where is my phone again?
Where the fuck is my drink?"
Now I've had a couple beers
and I am a little fucking high,
and people keep asking stupid questions
while I just try to hide inside my mind.
I don't want to make any more decisions.
Everything is fucking fine.
I thank you for your concern
but please leave me alone at this time.
Shit, I forgot to turn on the dryer.
"Where are the earrings I just bought her?"
"What do I put on the list?"
"How are the kids?"
"How is your father?"
I don't know. I can't call mom and ask her.

Jai K

JODIE BENDER S.B.

MY ARMOR

Years ago, I took my armor off and gently set it aside, hoping never to need it again.
It has many scratches and dents, and a few rusty spots in the shape of teardrops.
However, it still offers me the same protection it always has.
I'm a different shape now than I was way back then,
but every once in a while, I slip it on, and somehow it fits perfectly still.
Although I shouldn't ever need it again, I just can't seem to let it go.
Parting with it would feel as if I'm abandoning an old friend.
It comforts me to know it's there whenever, or if ever, I should be called into battle again.

Jodie Bender

I THOUGHT SHE'D BE FINE

She told us she was sick on a day late in November.
It was a heartbreaking day I will always remember.

Stage four Breast Cancer, the words you never want to hear.
I was filled with so many emotions: love, hope, dismay, and fear.
I knew this was serious, but in my mind, I thought she'd be fine;
after all, women beat this evil cancer all the time.

She started her chemo, and never once did she complain.
She lost all her hair, but it didn't bother her; she wasn't vain.
The chemo was aggressive; on her body, it took such a toll.
Her energy, her skin, and her memory, so much it stole.
I knew this was serious, but in my mind, I thought she'd be fine;
after all, women beat this evil cancer all the time.

It beat her down, and she was so sick, so tired, so weak,
Things were not looking good; her future looked bleak.
Then she got a little better, and my hope was renewed.
I thought she'd be fine, and my fears were subdued.
I knew this was serious, but in my mind, I thought she'd be fine;
after all, women beat this evil cancer all the time.

I was sitting at a restaurant when I got the call,
The words I hated to hear, the words that changed it all.
The cancer had spread; it now invaded her brain,
At that moment, I knew in my soul, and my heart was slain.
Her health deteriorated quickly after that horrible day.

*Six months after being diagnosed, she lost her battle at the end of
May.*
Cancer took my hero, my Mother, my beautiful friend.
And left a hole in my heart, which will never mend.

Jodie Bender

MY MONSTERS

As a child, I would have prayed for my monsters to be in the closet or under the bed.
To be figments of my imagination, not real, but just thoughts in my head.
The afflictions they caused still haunt me, though I'm much older.
Crushing my tortured soul like a massive jagged boulder.
There are times I swear I see those monsters in a stranger's leer,
And my entire being becomes paralyzed with overwhelming fear.
Yes, I will forever belong to those monsters; my soul is theirs to keep.
No, my scars will never be beautiful, for they run just way too deep.

Jodie Bender

SHAUNA WOODBURY

FOR THIS VIEW

Coming over the concrete rise, I see the early morning city lights. I stare down into the valley of your crowded circus. You're somewhere down this roadside slide, deep in a self-induced haze, with a vodka tonic in one hand and a Xanax cocktail in the other. Your hair smells like fire, and your green eyes, watery with a hangover, dance in pain under the dimming street lights.

Are you alone?

I've walked all night to see this view. The beautiful skyscape glares at me as it kisses the tip of this hill I stand on.

I'm battleworn.

My feet cry in agony.
I've walked all night to see this view.
You have no idea I'm here.
I've no idea why I'm here.

The highway is stained with years of travellers and wanderers, and the skyline is ribbons of burnt pink trailing away as dawn's fog lifts. It's quiet up here. I'm too far away to hear the torture and screams living so close to you causes.

You're ridiculous, a wreck.

A parasite.

Why did I come back?

You're like a dirty addiction. I can run, but I'm never free.
I stare down this hill into your hideous waking trap.
The trees line the road, and birds fly high.
I walked all night to see this view.
I take one step towards your horrible life.
All our history screams at me to turn back.
Not one stride further.
I walked all night to see this view.
Somewhere among the sounds and smells you sit, not knowing I'm here.

My pace has quickened.

I need to get there.

Where?

City limit sign.

I stop.

This is the definitive moment.

I breathe deeply before I enter your realm and suck in your poison.

Forward on.

Sidewalks and fences, vacant gravel lots, and broken windows scattered for miles, it seems. People asleep under boxes and cars on blocks without wheels.
I walked all night to see this view.
I can feel your damage, empathy from such a distance. The black ooze from the infection you label love has filmed over my skin.

As Darkness Falls

A man I used to know waves at me; he points up to a broken window of a brick building.

I'm afraid to look up.

I might see you.

Worse.

I might want you to love me.

Maybe I want you dead.

The same man who waved pisses on the side of the wall all over the bricks.

I walked all night to see this view.

I hear a window above me slide open, and bits of rocks and red brick with flecks of paint dust fall to the ground.

Oh fuck, it's you.

Your hair, wild and streaky, with peroxided stripes, blows its crawling inhabitants in the morning breeze. You empty beer bottles onto the street, yelling unintelligible rants. I shield my eyes from the sun to see you clearer.

A cigarette hangs off your lips, clinging by the mung that's grown on your morning mouth.

I cringe.

Vomit rises in my throat.

Stop.

I push it back.

I walked all night for this view.

You stop your swearing and raspy cum filled throaty laugh and look down as you hear the guy who pees on walls yell "hey! Blow job?"

You see me and ignore him. Your mouth drops open, and the lit cigarette falls into the piss. You hold your heap of hair up and say, "holy shit, what do you want?"

I don't know the answer.

I walked all night for this view.

I don't have a reason.

The silence is loud.

The man zips up his pants and starts yelling about reunions and old times.

You and I have nothing to say.

We just stare at each other.

Time stops.

I break the lock and look away. When I look back up, you're not there, and the window is closed.

I look directly at the building door expecting it to open. It doesn't.

You've made your statement. I turn to walk.

The street is a ghost town. The vampires and whores are sleeping the morning away.

As Darkness Falls

Where am I going?

A drink?

Yes.

Tavern of shit ahead. Why not.

I sit at the bar in the tavern, local guy next to me shaking his head. He asks, "why did you come back?"

I had nothing to say.

I stared at him. I wondered if he had fucked you too.

I left the tavern and ran back to your building. I threw pieces of garbage and rocks at your window.

Nothing happened.

Where did you go?

I turned away. This was a waste of time.

Why had I made this journey?

I still didn't know.

This was about four days ago.

Here I sit in my home writing this to you and telling you of my story. You never wanted to know my story. So many times I tried to tell you.

I hope this letter finds you well.

I had so much to tell you and nothing to say.

You could've taken just a moment to see me.

I'm your only son, and today I marry my husband. You never listened.

Now I accept you never wanted me.

I stare into my man's eyes today and realize why I walked all night for that view.

To say goodbye.

I love you, Mom.

Shauna Woodbury

CLINT DAVIS

SORRY MOM

The growling in front of him had been constant but switches to a frenzied bark. His eight-year-old mind thinks about his mom. The last thing she said to him when he left for school was, "I love you." He wishes he'd have said it back, instead of just, 'OK mom, gosh.' He wanted to tell her now, so very much.

Sorry, Mom.

Even though it's the last days of August here in south Texas, Joey's frozen in place. This ain't like any other dog he's seen before. This one's ugly. Dad calls dogs like this "mangy". If dad was here, he'd just shoot it, and they'd go home.

Home. Right past T.J.'s yard. If I get over the first fence, maybe this mangy mutt can't follow. He moves, but the growling and barking speeds up and turns nasty with slobber. Joey's eyes well up with tears, and he can't stop it. He wants to see his mom so bad. His backpack feels so heavy.

Wait.

He slowly dips his shoulders, one at a time, and the pack slides into the crook of his elbows, just like he's practiced a hundred times before. Who would've thought wanting to learn to shed that backpack while running to his room after school could've been so helpful now? Especially since his mom always yelled at him for leaving it in the hallway.

"Sorry, Mom," Joey yells as he flings the pack at the mangy mutt and turns, speeding for the first fence between him and home. The dog lunges, but Joey only hears the barking because he never looks back.

This first fence was barbed wire and separated T.J.'s yard from the pasture. The pasture he is not supposed to be in. Again.

Sorry, Mom.

The boys had been over this fence a million times, and through the tears, Joey smiles and jumps.

At first, he couldn't understand why his shoe came off. Then, he sees the ground rushing toward his face. He's tripped over the top strand, too late to catch himself. His arms flail out, and his face plants in the hard dirt and grass. The rest of his body crumples to the ground at nearly the same time. He lets out a muffled cry, curling up. The last time Joey felt something like this, a baseball slammed into his nose. Then he hears the growling, louder than ever, and he's up and running for the second fence.

Now, along with tears, Joey feels something heavy and sticky running past his mouth and down his chin.

He spits out what tastes like a dirty penny. His face throbs, and his legs are heavy. The urge to look back causes Joey to slow down. The barking and growling speed him up. The last fence is close. Then a dirt road. Then his front porch. Then home. He pushes forward without his pack and only one shoe.

Sorry, Mom.

Joey jumps, grabbing the top post of the chain-link fence and cries out, his hand suddenly on fire from one of the wires sticking up, but he doesn't stop. He can't. He has to see his mom again. The foot with the shoe plants in the middle of the fence, and he pushes up and flips, tumbling feet over head, landing on his back.

And losing all his breath.

Crying, bloody, throbbing, hand on fire, and still can't breathe, Joey doesn't move. The dog slams against the fence, barking and snapping. Joey flinches and rolls into the dirt road.

The barking and growling forces Joey to get up and he stands frozen in the blazing heat once more, eyes squeezed shut. Shaking, crying, and bleeding, he listens to the monster tearing through the fence.

Imagining its teeth ripping into his body, Joey lets out the breath he must've been holding with a loud snort. Bloody, tear-filled snot shoots out.

When nothing happens but more barking and fence slamming, he opens his eyes. The mangy, ugly mutt is doing its best to tear up the fence to get at Joey. His face hurts. And his hand hurts. And he wants to see his mom.

Joey turns away, stumbling towards his porch. When he reaches the bottom of the steps, he can't hear the fence rattling anymore. But the barking and growling is getting louder. He jumps up the three steps and grabs the doorknob, turning it.

It doesn't open. Mom's not home yet. He reaches for the key attached to his backpack, the pack that's in the pasture. Joey hears the mangy monster louder than ever now. He slumps his shoulders, and at eight years old, Joey turns around to meet his fate. He isn't crying anymore.

"Sorry, Mom," Joey whispers.

Clint Davis

WHISKEY HELL

"I walk dead or alive; I waste my time whenever I like" – Godsmack

There is nothing pretty about regret.

It's even worse when you can't save the life of your own child. I keep hearing time will make the sting fade away. Some say it'll never fade. This knife in my chest day after day. It turns in my heart hour after hour.

A red '89 Firebird slams into my little boy every minute of my existence. I run as fast as I can every time, but I never make it.

"Nooooo!" Falling to my knees, second after second.

I've heard about Hell. About burning in a lake of fire. I'd welcome it. The whiskey burned at first.

There's nothing there now. I couldn't even call it numb. I pour it down my throat. I have no idea how long it's been since I've actually eaten. The liquid that fills my gut works fine. I don't fucking care.

I deserve this. Sucked as a father anyway. I stayed at work when I should've come home to play. He always asked me to play. Always too busy tinkering. Or on my phone. Or drinking. Or not paying attention.

I didn't pay attention three days ago. Daydreaming about work. He darted ahead of me and out in the street. A woman screamed. I ran. And fell to my knees.

I'm still falling.

I take another swig. "At least I won't fall anymore." My finger traces the smooth, cool metal of the service Glock forty. I've never had to use it at work. Only shot for practice. I only need to fire it once more. I'd give anything to see my boy again. This is my only option.

The barrel is cold against my teeth, but I bite down. I don't need it to slip. I close my eyes, and I see the car hit him again. Tears leak down my face. I'll get to see him again soon. Or I'll burn. Either way, I'll stop falling.

The pounding at the door makes me flinch, and I jerk the gun out of my mouth. I'm hyperventilating. My heart pounds heavier than the fist at the door.

My partner. "Open the fucking door!"

Terminator Voice. "Fuck you. Asshole." I shove the pistol between the couch cushions but take another pull of whiskey.

The door swings open, and Tommy barrels through. "Tha fuck you been? You turned your phone off." He stops and cringes. "Jesus, you look like shit and smell worse."

I take another drink.

He grabs the bottle and tosses it off to the side. "We gotta go! Your boy's awake!"

Clint Davis

LISA PILGRIM

DEAD END

On those rare occasions
when I am able to step
outside my pride, I cross
paths with the harsh
reality of my actions.

Choosing the dark route
when I found myself at
that fork. Unwilling to make
a U-Turn, and falsely believing
the unknown to be a paradise
destination.

Through the rearview mirror
of my soul, I navigate the
cracks left in your heart.
Never realizing it wasn't
made of concrete, or that
it would lead to a dead end.

Lisa Pilgrim

FROZEN

Quivering as the ice-cold breeze brushes the back of my bare neck where sultry lips once met skin.

Frigid air burns my lungs as I struggle to remember the warmth of his bare chest pressed against my naked breasts.

Kneeling on frozen ground before the slab of granite that bears remembrance of the details of the life of the man whose passion could melt a cemetery gate.

Mourning the man who now slumbers beside strangers, rather than in my arms, as I struggle to keep my shivering heart from freezing.

Lisa Pilgrim

ACCEPTANCE

Limping down to the river's edge,
maneuvering through the sharp,
slippery, rocks of my memories
I sit sifting through the ashes
of the bridge you burned,
searching for understanding.
Dusting the soot from the hands
that long to hold you,
I realize this darkness won't soon wash off.

The fire that was us burned white-hot
on promises and good intentions.
It's going to take years and tears to clean
the sediment that now stains my charred
heart with no answers to scrub it.

But, you never know,
if I have enough faith
and I don't give up,
maybe
somewhere in this devastation
I will find acceptance.

Lisa Pilgrim

BRANDIE WHALEY

PONDER

I ponder, ponder, one step short of full-on obsession. Mulling over the world I grew up in and how suddenly and without fanfare, it ceased to exist. So unexpected and lightning-quick its flame burnt out that I don't think most people understand that they are living in an extinct age. I wonder if they realize they are living remnants, someone's archaic example of what life was like before the world moved on. These thoughts run circuitous paths wearing imaginable indentations on the surface of my over-wrought brain....searching for a solution that doesn't exist to answer a problem no one acknowledges as fact. Fairy-tale supplication rides this mental mystery machine alongside undoubted fact, one cloaked in the shadow of the other to where in the distance they are interchangeable, two almost melding into one with the right squint of an eye.

This doubling is indicative of the larger topic at hand, eerie proof that truth is subjective, based more on perception and perspective than any of us feel comfortable admitting out loud.

My musings go far, covering as much of my personal truth as my mind can conjure. I ponder, ponder, and ponder some more, trying to pinpoint when this world began to evolve into the nightmare dreamscape that it has now become. I look at those around me, faces I know almost as well as my own, and wonder if their inner landscape mirrors their increasingly strange outerscape. I wonder if they are familiar strangers, awkward doppelgangers unsure how to act in the skin they're posing in.

I compare the world I knew as a child, raised in the faith of my father's, secure in the belief of a God that made me, a God that loved me, a God that never strayed far from me.

I think of that child I was, of the fears I had to contend with, and I compare that to the children that have now come from me, of the dangers they have had to face, and of the fears I, as a child, could not even fathom, much less comprehend. I wonder where my God went when I wasn't looking ... I wonder when a child's innocent fear of the dark was made to include whatever evils might accompany the darkness, and it is beyond my ability to process. I wonder when evil acts committed by evil men became commonplace in a now evil world, and why am I the only voice I hear, crying out against the darkness.

Is this how it ends for us, imperfect beings created and set loose to do as we would, an experiment begun in the hope that we would embody the love that we were formed of, living representations of flawed incomplete souls striving to emulate the loving God whose image we were cast in, instead we have fallen further than the furthest fallen of the outcast. Will we be the abominations that so many of us have allowed ourselves to become.

I ponder, ponder, one step short

Of full-on obsession.

Brandie Whaley

SANDCASTLES

Your life is a lie-
A sandcastle built
Perilously close to
The high tide line.
A mirage, camouflaged
To look like reality,
But is nothing more than a fragile illusion...
Always in danger
Of crumbling back into nothing
At the crash of each new wave.

All the tools you used
To create this pleasing facade-
The hope that became your roof,
The joy that formed your walls,
The love that you poured out
As your foundation-
Are all tied up and holding together
Something that is as temporary
And uncertain as time itself.

You became so enchanted, so entranced,
By the illusion
That you eventually forgot
That what you were creating
Was as fleeting and insubstantial
As a ghost.
And now you discover that everything

185

As Darkness Falls

You've held onto,
Everything you've believed to be true,
All the love you kept close,
Held deep down inside of you,
All the markers that you
Used to define you,
Were never anything more
Than intricately designed sandcastles,
Waiting to be washed back out to sea.

Brandie Whaley

DIANA THOMAS | JUMPED UP

SHADOW CHILD

On shaking and trembling legs, she stood and stared down at the sheet with the smears of blood that had been her innocence.

Too weary to run, she stumbled into her dark bedroom closet and shut the door. She was terrified but found solace and comfort within those tiny dark four walls. The house had fallen quiet from her screams and his drunken grunting and swearing.

She doesn't remember how long she hid in the closet, but it was dusk when she exited. Although her body ached, and her mind was dull, she felt hyper-vigilant.

She gathered all her strength and wits about her, stripped her bed, and quietly tiptoed through the house. With the sheets and bloodied clothes in the washer, she grabbed clean clothes and panties and locked herself in the bathroom. She showered, scrubbing herself raw. Her eyes peered out of the shower curtain repeatedly, making sure she had locked the door.

Exiting the shower, she noticed that the bleeding between her legs had slowed some, but it had not stopped completely. So she packed her panties with two pads and dressed herself in baggy pants and an oversized long sleeve shirt. The shower had been steaming hot, but she was chilled to the bone. Her skin tingled, but she still felt dirty, unclean. She listened through the bathroom door for any sounds, but thankfully the only thing she could hear was his drunken snoring coming from his bedroom.

She quietly snuck out of the bathroom and quickly locked herself in her bedroom. She remade her bed and curled up under her blanket, but she felt no comfort. Her soul was as cold as ice, and her mind was trying to grasp hold of what happened. She softly cried, wondering what she should do, what should she say, should she tell anyone, or would she say or do nothing. She remembered him telling her to keep her slutty mouth shut. He had warned her, cursed at her, and threatened her.

Terrible and crazy thoughts entered her head. This was her fault; somehow she had deserved it. She remembered his drunken words telling her exactly that. She was ugly, fat, and he had said no one would ever love her. Hell, he had said that her own father had abandoned her and that this act had been his right because, after all, it was him that was feeding her, housing her, and supporting her.

She slept fitfully that night, waking often in trembling fear, but by morning she had decided she would not tell. She would never tell because, in reality, who would believe her...

Diana Thomas (Jumped Up)

EMMA GLEDHILL

SHATTERED INNOCENCE

I have seen Hell; I lived there for a while.
Bereft of hope, I spent years without a smile.
An innocent heart, now broken beyond repair,
A haunted mind, shattered by despair.

Emma Gledhill

DISCARDED HOPE

The clouds crossed the moon, and the wind blew without care for its
effect, as my heart sat empty,
devoid of emotion and all hope of love forsaken.
Giving up was all that was left. Loneliness was all that was felt.

Emma Gledhill

ELIZABETH

AS QUOTED

"One day you'll find your soulmate…"
Bullshit! There's no such thing.
What you find is another human being
who has been hurt and broken down just as much
as you, and figured out how to survive, vowing to
never treat another in the same manner that
damaged them.
They are the ones who have discovered
that life is humbling
and love is healing.
They will guard you,
as much as they guard themselves.
Do not seek the perfect,
for they do not know their meaning;
seek the faltered,
for they have much to teach.

elizabeth

PREYED UPON

Weaving intricate conversations
with a forced smile,
you intrigue another woman.
Her suspicions unformed,
she is captivated by your unknown –
fixed in the scheme.
Confrontation.
She notices detail.
Your dark and mysterious eyes…
…are like two-way mirrors
and through any angled light,
a shadow is cast.
Elaboration.
Such a foudroyant life you've created.
In the beginning, there are no questions,
no doubts.
We are understanding.
Ahhh! The slip of your forgetful tongue.
Do you remember which thoughts –
lust and desire…passion and position –
you shared with whom?
Internally you struggle,
"Is she the one? (Shrug) Guess."
You grin mischievously inside.
Hidden deep within your subconscious,
you are aware,
aren't you?

As Darkness Falls

Coward!!
Blatant displays of your make-believe
fantasies – this is your reality,
lost within your fenced perimeter of mind.
Your paint-by-number picture
is shattered – she figures out the game.
You start over; the cycle begins,
again...
preyed upon.

elizabeth

TIME

Time does not really stand still,
but the mind can stall years at will
Each grain of sand slipping through the glass
is yet another second gone from our grasp

Slowly collecting in the bottom half of our lives
are memories cherished from days gone by
Fading are the negative thoughts, while
remembering stories with twisted plots
Reminiscing preserved family histories and
passing down traditional legacies

The sands of time seem infinite in mass,
until they're held in your hourglass
Watching your time slip through your hands
while turning the glass over and over again

Memories breaking apart with each revolution
never fitting back together with complete absolution
Mindful of time spread out over an eternity,
collect your grains so meticulously
For one second, one minute, one day will pass,
unrecovered from your hour glass

elizabeth

JANA BEGOVIC

MUSINGS UPON A RIVER

The river flowed with faceless indifference,
In a rhythm that seemed to be
Chiseled into time and space.
The crests and troughs of its waves,
Reminded him of his life, of its swells,
Buoyancy of passion, growth, and bliss, and
Its plummets into despair and dissolution.
Memories coloured with melancholy
Rose before his spiritual eye and
Gazing at the river,
He felt the inexorable hand of time
Emptying out his moments
In the direction of no return.

Jana Begovic

GRAVEYARD

In the graveyard of discarded lovers,
Unspoken words, betrayals and
Broken wows,
Among the love whispers,
Turned to hauntings, and
Memories gnawed away,
By the transience of time,
My heart still throbs your name
In crimson red.

Jana Begovic

TAPESTRY OF LIFE

The bitter salt of grief and tears,
The honey taste of joyous years,
The aching echo of absences,
The ebb and flow of gains and losses,
The love that came as heaven cloaked,
The portal to hell it soon evoked,
The unbottled longings hurled at the moon,
The dragonfly days when in love we swoon,
The charcoal fear making the soul cry,
The effervescent dreams that still ride high.

Jana Begovic

BRIAN BERRYMAN

PERMANENT GOODBYE

I think back to the past
Of days gone before
And it conjures you
You're outside my door
You say that you've changed
Like you always do
You want to start over
Begin things anew
There may have been good times
But there was so many more bad
You left me broken
Taking all that I had
It's time
Time for a permanent goodbye
You said you loved me
But your lies said otherwise
I gave, and I gave
Until I couldn't give more
Do I really want you

Back outside my door?
All the gaslighting
And all of the pain
Will it be different

As Darkness Falls

Or more of the same?
It's time
Time for a permanent goodbye
You said you wanted me
But your actions said otherwise
Promises broken
Far too many to list
Will I be tempted
Or will I resist?
The lying, the cheating
Never true to your word
And when I called you on it
My voice went unheard
It's time
Time for a permanent goodbye
You said you needed me
But your deeds said otherwise
I'm all out of tears
I have none left to cry
So I think that its best
For a Permanent Goodbye
It's time
Time for a permanent goodbye

Brian Berryman

OUTSIDE LOOKING IN

Concerned
Cannot think of anything
Except you
Spinning my cigarette lighter
Between my fingers and thumb
In my pocket like it's a worry stone
Spinning
Spinning
Over and over and over and over
Standing outside
In the cold
Wishing I wasn't on the Outside
Looking in
Quite so much
I want to help, but I cannot
I just want to be able to
Do anything to help
Make this hellish nightmare end for you
But all I can do is stand here
Worried sick
Outside in the cold
Looking in
Feeling so utterly fucking helpless

Brian Berryman

WE SHALL CONTINUE ON

I write this as I sit in my brother's home in Vermont, reconciling his estate after his passing. As I write, I am realizing that life is so short, and that time, although it constantly and consistently marches forward, does not do so with us. Time is not obligated to us, nor does it care one whit for us. It continues. We do not.

I think of all these things as I look about at all the laid plans, all the hopes and dreams of my brother, never accomplished, never completed. And I think to myself, who?

Who will pick up this banner where he fell?

Who will accomplish the tasks he began?

Who will pick up the banner when I fall?

Who will complete my tasks?

I have my own private kingdom...my own little universe. To accomplish the tasks of those before me, alongside my own, has become impossible. I feel I cannot do it all, but I must continue. As who else will pick up that banner?

Who will tend the garden when he is gone?

Who will tend the garden when I am gone?

Someone will.

We are an industrious bunch, humans. There is always someone to take over. Their hopes and dreams may not align with our own, but they will, unwittingly or not, pick up the banner of humanity and continue.

And they shall march through their time until the banner is passed yet again.

We shall continue on. And time cannot take that away from us. As long as we remember those who came before us, and their hopes and dreams, they, and we, shall endure.

And that is the hope for this great World.

Brian Berryman

SLV

FEAR

I fear I am here
in this dark and cold hole,
burrowing in the ground for warmth.
In angst.
The howling, cold wind
is slicing through me,
stripping pieces of me off,
discarding them like last week's trash.
I'll never put me back together again.
I am raw.
I am exposed.
And I am too broken.

SLV

I KNOW NOW

I always thought that death come from trauma.
An accident
A heart attack
A fall
I never knew death comes from within.
Like swallowing acid
It slowly eats away at you
from the inside out
necrotic pieces soughing off here and there,
until all that's left
is rotting flesh and bone.
I know now

SLV

LITTLE PIECES

You fall apart slowly, you know. Little pieces of your life dropping off you, leaving a trail of heartache and pain everywhere you go. Your DNA paints this town with tears over here, empty promises over there, and a pile of broken dreams collecting dust in the corner. And you're standing there empty and naked, with only vulnerability draping your shoulders. That's when the vultures come. They'll strip what's left in your withering soul, and wipe their mouths with the end of your tattered heart.

SLV

STEPHANIE BENNETT-HENRY

GO BACK

If I could go back, I would take all the wrong turns on purpose. I would be reckless with chances, and greedy with wishes. I would believe in more, but trust less.

If I could go back, I would find my fears early and kick their asses sooner. I would realize that eye contact never killed anyone, and words hurt, but silence is what breaks hearts.

I would go back to tell myself that I have the sky in my eyes, the universe in my heart, and dynamite built into my bare feet.

I would tell that beautiful girl not to ever let anyone crack her steel spine, never let anyone slip disregard under her nail beds, and never let anyone leave a trail of regret under her skin and call it a promise.

I wold tell her to always remember who's writing her story.

Stephanie Bennett-Henry

WAR

All of this time, it looked as though I was doing nothing at all, but just beneath the calm, hiding behind the peaceful facade that was sometimes smiling, make no mistake....

I was at war with myself.

Battling demons, digging up skeletons, fighting the ghosts that still haunt me. Laying the worst parts of me down into their final resting place, throwing dirt on all the wounds that would not heal.

And I am done.

Throw every white flag in the air; I finally won.

Conquering your own war is the hardest thing you'll ever do, but looking in your own eyes when it's all over and loving yourself is a priceless victory you cannot look away from.

Stephanie Bennett-Henry

MY LIGHT

I have apologized for not being good enough too many times and it took me a long time to realize that the ones I said sorry to were not worthy of even touching my light.

And if you ever find yourself apologizing for your dark, please remember that your dark is only too much for the ones who have yet to conquer their own.

Stephanie Bennett-Henry

JAY LONG

SHATTERED HORIZONS

The dreams I went chasing
have been set adrift in the dark waters of hopelessness.
All the pieces that connect now to then
have taken their rightful place
at the bottom of an endless well of wishes.
Eternity will not pardon me from a single moment's madness.
My horizons have shattered.
They are now just shredded parts of my tomorrows
that lay recklessly strewn about the shoreline
like ripped out pages of a book of unanswered prayers.

Jay Long

THE DARKNESS

Leave the lights on,
it's much easier to find them,
the demons that call me home.
I've grown tired of the shadows,
lost touch with the darkness.
In my proudest moments
they sit beside me to steal the spotlight.
They feed on fear
and live on the insecurities
created through years of self-doubt.
So leave the lights on there is no reason to hide.
For I am my demons and I no longer run.

Jay Long

ABOUT THE AUTHORS

C.N. GREER

Growing up in the Pacific Northwest, C.N. Greer has never been lacking in inspiration. In the last twenty years, she has taken that inspiration and expressed it for the world through the written word. An avid book reader, C.N. Greer is a fantasy writer and a poet. She hopes to share that love of fiction with her daughter. When she's not writing, she's spending time with her family and wrangling the fur babies that keep her life interesting. She believes in the human spirit and a person's capacity for strength and resilience, but she also knows those virtues can be hard won. She is an advocate for equality and compassion, and she hopes to bring some light into this world with her work of poetry and prose. Follow her

facebook.com/cngreerpoetry | instagram.com/cngreerpoetry

LISA PILGRIM

Lisa Pilgrim is a self-described scribbler of sentences, a weaver of words, and a teller of tales. Lisa writes of love, lust, longing, loss, life, and throws in a pinch of laughter every now and again. A Southern Belle who has mapped the streets of hell, Lisa openly shares her victories and her losses through poetry and prose as she believes words are the conduit that connects us all.

Follow on Facebook at facebook.com/pricelesswords1

JESSICA MILLER

Born and raised in Northern Michigan, Jessica Miller currently puts pen to paper in Colorado Springs, Colorado, where she works as a CNA and Massage Therapist. She was raised in a Conservative Mennonite Church, but left that setting when she was 21 to chase her dream of being in the healthcare field. Through poetry, she offers a closer look at betrayal, loss, heartache, compassion, love, hope, and survival. Somewhere between Northern Michigan and Colorado, she found herself gasping for oxygen, and the new life that the fresh mountain air breathed into her dying soul, is the same life that she uses to speak her truth today. Jessica's hope is that her voice and her story will be used as a beacon of hope, to spiritual, sexual, and domestic violence survivors everywhere. It is her wish that not only this, but all future generations of young girls and women will be as fierce in their determination and use their stories and voices to speak up for those who cannot speak for themselves. Follow her on Facebook at facebook.com/rediscoveryofwonder and @rediscoveryofwonder on Instagram

RUBY JANE PRIAS (JDG)

Ruby Jane Prias is a Physics Teacher that loves to introduce different ideas on how young learners will enjoy learning. Born and raised to appreciate everything in life. She loves to write in every situation that she's in, every feeling that she has. She usually spends her free time writing to express her emotions.
facebook.com/janeprias | instagram.com/Ihavej

ASTRID S.

Astrid S lives in Texas in the USA. She is the eldest of 3 and is a puppy wrangler and cat whisperer. Her cat Jackson likes to keep an eye on her to make sure that he gets his fair share of her attention. She loves school, swimming and playing the violin. When she has time, she likes to bake for her family. She writes poetry, short stories and is writing her first novel. Astrid enjoys writing and long video calls to her aunt (also a writer) in Cape Town, South Africa. In the few hours that they are awake at the same time, they talk for ages about writing, mythology and how similar they are (despite a 33 year age gap). Astrid is excited to realise her dream of being published in this anthology and feels that this is the beginning of a long and fulfilling writing journey.

SLV

SLV is a Canadian writer and poet. For more of their writing visit facebook.com//sweetSherriLee

GRACEFULLY BROKEN

Guil Joseph is simply a man who wants to have a great relationship with all the people surrounding him. He gives smile to everyone in the dark and cloudy days of life. His writings were inspired by someone who is very special to him.

facebook.com/creativelybroken | instagram.com/gracefullybrokenjdg

CHARLENE ANN BENOIT

Charlene Ann Benoit, a native of Newfoundland, Canada, began writing poetry at the age of ten. In 2004, she finished her first collection of poems, entitled, Pieces of My Soul. In 2005, she completed her first novel, When Walls Come Crashing Down. Since that time, she has compiled five other books of poetry: In Memory Of (2005), Shattered (2008), Between the Lines (2019), In the Hearts of Gods, Monsters, and Men (2020) and Blood, Tears and Coffee Rings (2020). She has also written a children's book, The Littlest Prince (2015), that is currently on hold for illustrations. She released a short fictional memoir called Death's Daughter in 2020. The Skeptic, her second completed novel, is expected to be released early in the new year. Follow her on Facebook at facebook.com/charleneannbenoit

DAWN P. HARRELL

Dawn P. Harrell works full time and writes for fun and also for healing and hope. She tends toward darker pieces, but that's only because she writes exactly what she feels. She has a soft spot for abuse victims and those who struggle with their worth, as these are parts of her as well. Dawn lives in Southwest Mississippi and loves being outside. In her spare time, she likes to hang out with her 2 grown sons and daughter-in-law, as well as her 3 rescue dogs. She enjoys working in the yard, devouring books, and all things horror. She is shamelessly nerdy, a longtime lover of the night, and you can find her at 3 am looking at the stars and contemplating her next piece or watching classic horror movies. Her debut book, Seasons of a Sewer Girl, is available through Amazon and all online booksellers Follow her on Facebook at facebook.com/seasonsofasewergirl | @sewergirl71 on Instagram | linktr.ee/DawnPHarrell

LORNA HUSBAND

Lorna is an avid reader, bibliophile, devoted cat mom and nature lover. Born and raised in the Great Lake State, she is drawn to water and enjoys the changing seasons. As an amateur photographer, wildlife and natural landscapes are her favorite subject matter. She began writing for personal pleasure at the age of ten, but after college the creative urge was pushed aside while pursuing other goals. In recent years she has found the urge to pick up the pen again and she believes everyone has at least one good poem in them if they can listen to their heart and let the words flow.
instagram.com/bridgesnotburnt

D. RODGERS

D. Rodgers, aka Plucky Em, has been through a lot these past few years, but has never given up her fighting spirit. She is currently living in one of the most beautiful mountain states in the US. Her home is filled with many children, including two fur babies. From an early age, she has always had a love for writing. She is an accomplished poet, hoping to publish her own works in the near future taking others on her healing journey through poetry. It is her desire that her writing will touch readers who have survived trauma, giving them hope and healing, as she has found.
facebook.com/PluckyEm | instagram.com/thewritingsofpluckyem/

ELIZABETH

Howling Wolf Poetry is penned by elizabeth. The daughter of a self-proclaimed Grammar Queen and an artistic outdoorsman known for his watercolor paintings, elizabeth has been writing poetry for over 30 years – unbeknownst to most people in her life – until now. She has artists of different mediums on both sides of her family; some incredibly famous, and some just really good at what they do. With encouragement found in online writing and poetry groups, she began to reveal what only she had known – parts of herself and others in words of Life, Love, Loss, and Lust. Born and raised in California between the mountains and the ocean, she spends as much time caressing the earth as she does the keyboard. Her tolerance is high, her temper is low, and her love of animals and people is wider than any compass can measure. Follow her facebook.com/howlingwolfpoetry | instagram.com/hwlgwlf_poetry

JENNIFER JENNINGS DAVES

A relative newcomer, Jennifer Daves is finding her place in the world of social media writers. However, she is not limiting her capabilities and is working to stretch her talents to the farthest reaches. Jennifer's writing is as often playful as it is brutal. Two sides of a completely complex and beautiful soul - one that invites you into the garden for tea but warns you of the dangers of sitting too close to the rose bushes, as she plucks the bloody thorns from her heart, one by one, and offers them to you. Whether it is prose, poetry or a song, she will definitely capture your attention as she serves up delicate pieces of her soul. Follow her iworeabraforthis.com | facebook.com/snapandflingitoff

STEPHANIE MUELLER

Stephanie Mueller is a certified elementary school teacher in bilingual and bi-cultural education. In addition to teaching, she enjoys exploring her passion for words and poetry. Through a deep connection with animals and nature, she often finds inspiration for her writing by simply observing the quiet moments around her. Stephanie fills her days in Wisconsin with her daughter and two fur-babies. She soaks up the summer sunshine in her garden and spends the evenings taking walks and chasing fireflies. As Stephanie continues to fulfill her life's calling, she hopes to inspire loving-kindness and compassion for all living beings. Connect with Stephanie, samuellerblog.wordpress.com | facebook.com/mueller.stephanie.827 | instagram.com/stephaniemueller827

AMY PASZTAS

Amy has self-published three books to date in the poetry/prose genre and is working on branching out and attempting a novel. She currently resides in Tennessee with her three and a half dogs (a yorkie only counts as half) where she recently moved to be closer to her parents. Amy's love for travel and nature photography, combined with her love of reading keep her imagination active. After all, sometimes we each have to create our own magic. Follow her on Facebook at facebook.com/PasztasA

EMILY JAMES

Emily James is the pseudonym used by Lori Weyandt. Lori's soul roams from the mountains of Pennsylvania to the mountains of North Carolina. She shares her life with her fiancé Brian, her daughter Kirsten, son-in-law Gage and her littlest love, her granddaughter Miss Elliott Rose. facebook.com/akaemilyjames | instagram.com/akaemilyjames

NICOLE LABONTE

Nicole has been writing since the early age of ten!
She is now a single mom to a nine year old daughter and works in the beauty industry full time. Nicole has self published her first novel, titled 'The Wand' which is the first of a trilogy, and has contributed to a few different anthologies. She is a dedicated mom, aunt, and friend, with dedication and ambition to follow her dreams.
Nicole has an extreme passion for animals, music and poetry, she loves to write short stories. facebook.com/NicoleLabontewriter

SHAWNA OLIBAMOYO

Shawna has dabbled in writing from an early age but it wasn't until 2014 that her poetry really came to life. It was a very challenging year which included a partial amputation of her right leg. As the words poured out, they became her escape and her therapy. Shawna really enjoys writing poetry and being able to express herself with every heartfelt word whether it be of love, pain or inspiration.

SHARMANI T. ADDERLEY

Sharmani T. Adderley is an educator, entrepreneur, poet, novelist living in Nassau, Bahamas. 'Track Road Through A Pine Forest' is her very first publication of selected works of poetry, self published via Amazon. Since then she has had her poems featured in the masterpiece 'Rise From Within'. What started out as a pastime has now become a passion as she currently has other works in progress. You can find her collective of poetry on Amazon.com. - facebook.com/trackr.forest | instagram.com/pineforest242

SUNNY WRIGHT

Sunny Wright is an up-and-coming poet blessed with the power of empathy which enables him to walk in the shoes of others and turn that into poetry. Loves to play with words and write in metaphors, usually writes about love and life, that of his own and the people around him. As Darkness Falls is his first appearance on paper as a poet. - facebook.com/SunnyWrightsPoetry

WILL HOEYE

Born in Sioux Falls, SD, Will Hoeye, is a relative new-comer. Though his works span almost 30 years, most were written since October 2020. With the creation of his Facebook page, "Force of Will," he started sharing his poetry. He writes from the heart, finding poetry to be his outlet; love, pain, loss, gain, and hope, all topics he has touched on. Currently living near St. Louis, he enjoys movies, music, reading, and the occasional bike ride. facebook.com/LordThrym77

BRANDY LANE

Brandy Lane is making a splash in the poetry world with the recent release of her new book "Where Beautiful Loves"(which is available on Amazon) and has been published in nearly a dozen anthologies within the past several months. She has become known in the Instagram world on several platforms for her passionate way of reading and interpreting poetry. She is working on her second book of poetry, and has big plans for the future, having started her own publishing LLC, Where Beautiful Inks. You can find Brandy on social media at the following: facebook.com/wherebeautifullives | instagram.com/wherebeautifullives/

GEORGE DELGADO

George Delgado is a writer and poet sharing his life's journey through words. For more check out fruitsofaddiction on Instagram

BRENDA CIERNIAK

Brenda Cierniak grew up in the heart of Lincolnshire in the UK. From an early age writing served as a form of therapy, helping express her emotions during a traumatic childhood, and continuing to do so through the trials of adult life. Words and their power always held a great fascination for Brenda, and poetry is an integral part of her soul. She writes from the heart, drawing on her own life experiences to write deeply personal, honest poetry encompassing; life, love, grief and mental health, with optimism and passion. Brenda's Facebook page to share her words was started in 2020, an Instagram page following the year after. She continues to live and write in her hometown, and hopes to connect with people through her poetry. facebook.com/sunshineandshadowspoet | instagram.com/sunshineandshadowspoet/

SHARIL MILLER

Sharil Miller is married with two beautiful daughters and three handsome grandsons. She loves photography as well as writing and tends to look at the world in a unique way capturing moments and memories not only through the lens, but through her pen as well. Sharil is adventurous and loves to travel. Three of her most favorite places for fun and adventures are Key West, The Outer Banks, and Myrtle Beach. She loves to go camping and has a cute retro camper to take time away to relax and refresh her soul. facebook.com/SharilLynMiller

VALERIE MESTA

Valerie Mesta considers herself an amateur writer who uses writing as an outlet for all of the emotional trauma she experienced through her life. Her story began before she could remember, and includes molestation, physical and mental abuse and rape. She often refers to abusers as monsters in her writing, and considers herself a warrior, not a survivor, because she's still fighting the demons of her past every day. Valerie suffers from PTSD, Bipolar, Anxiety, and Depression which comes through in her writing. While she often calls herself worthless, she believes that she's strong even in her weakest moment. Her writing is raw, honest, and full of rollercoaster emotions. She believes identifying is comforting and the key to helping others with similar issues simply feel human. Valerie's feels writing is her only voice and her ranting online is similar to screaming into a pillow.
Facebook.com/JustTakeMetotheTrees |
instagram.com/take_me_to_the.trees

B. VIGIL

Brianna Vigil, the small town girl from New Mexico is also known across the internet worldwide as the Dark Poetry Author, B. Vigil. She writes about the beauty in darkness, and love, and life, and pain, and everything in between. facebook.com/sheseesbeautyindarkness | bvigilauthor.onuniverse.com/

JODIE BENDER S.B.

An Ohio native, Jodie Bender was born an imperfectionist. She has always loved the idea that poetry does not always have to follow the rules. It does not always have to have structure; it can be chaotic and still be beautiful. As a child, she fell in love with and started writing poetry. She found emotional and spiritual strength in putting her feelings down on paper. Life got in the way, and she took a long hiatus from writing, however, with the tragedy of her cousin's long-term battle with brain cancer, she could not find any other way of expressing herself. She started writing again, and always looks back. Every person she meets affects her existence. She finds poetry in everyone and in everything that touches her. Bleeding to life, she writes every day; for better or for worse, Simply because she views the world as an endless poetic verse. – facebook.com/profile.php?id=100068843163448

BIZARRE MIZZ WILLIAMS

Creature to the grave, this body wont last forever and your vision will begin to fade. I pose for no man this woman ain't ever fake and you can't claim that I'm shady, because I don't run round the outside and I don't give a damn who hates me. Tell me for old times sake what it sounds like to spout lies and say that I'm self made, boy I'm hand made by all the love that raised me and the faith that carried me even when I went crazy. From day one the people that helped shape me couldn't make a mold I wouldn't break, but I thank the ones who staid because they're the ones that saved me. Love Always, The Bizarre Mizz Williams - facebook.com/unequivocally.yours

KELLI J GAVIN

Kelli J Gavin of Carver, Minnesota is a Writer, Editor, Blogger and Professional Organizer. With over 400 short stories and poems published and posted online, her work can be found with Clarendon House Publications, Sweetycat Press, Linden Books, The Ugly Writers, Zombie Pirates Publishing, Setu, 300 South Media Group, The Story Pub, Cut 19, Humans of Love, Otherwise Engaged, Flora Fiction, Margins Magazine, The Basil O'Flaherty, The Rye Whiskey Review, Some Good News, Sweatpants and Coffee, and Southwest Media among many others. Kelli's first two books were released in 2019 ("I Regret Nothing- A Collection of Poetry and Prose" and "My Name is Zach- A Teenage Perspective on Autism"). She has co-authored over 25 anthologies. "Stories I Should Have Written" will be published in 2021. She is also working on a collection of fiction short stories. kellijgavin.blogspot.com | @KelliJGavin on Twitter, Instagram and Facebook | @keltotheg on TikTok

STEPHANIE BENNETT-HENRY

Stephanie Bennett-Henry is a born and raised Texas based writer who shares her personal experiences through writing and poetry. Stephanie's ink flows eloquently, creating beauty with her words of motivation and inspiration to raise women up, no matter what stage of life they're in. Stephanie enjoys spending time with her husband and her son, as well as their 2 dogs, 2 cats, and 2 goats. Stephanie is currently writing her first book which will be available in early 2021 Follow her at facebook.com/poetryofSL & facebook.com/ragingrhetoric and stephaniebennetthenry & @ragingrhetoric on Instagram

LYSSA DAMON

Lyssa Damon lives in Cape Town, South Africa, in the heart of the winelands with her family and assortment of weird and wonderful pets. Lyssa has written in some form or another since she can remember, starting with a poem about kittens losing mittens in a puddle. She dabbles in poetry, short stories, flash fiction and is attempting to write a novel. She dreams of one day turning at least some of those stories into a screenplays. Lyssa loves the ocean, talks to moon and believes in magick. She loves animals and some people. Recently Lyssa has discovered that her niece, who lives in Texas, shares her love of writing. Despite the many miles between them, they video call often and talk about everything from puppies to Greek Mythology. She dreams of owning a castle with an enormous library where she can live, dream and write full time and invite niece for long visits. facebook.com/LinesByLyssa | instagram.com/LinesByLyssa

BIANCA MARIE NERY

Bianca Marie Nery is a 23-year-old writer and poet from the Philippines. She first started writing as a student journalist for her high school newspaper, going on to starting her poetry blog on WordPress in 2020. She published her first book, Letters From Quarantine, the same year. She currently lives in Manila with her family and two dogs. facebook.com/bmnpoetry | instagram.com/bncamarie/

MANDY KOCSIS

Born and raised on the streets of Detroit, Mandy Kocsis currently bleeds poetry from She Hates It Here, Indiana. She's the only surviving parent of her amazing teenage son. She's seen more darkness than most, and it often shows in her work. Where most see darkness, Mandy sees the light within. She lives there. She writes there. And, someday, she hopes to find that love really does exist, but for now she's a non-believer. Legally deaf since birth, she's trying desperately to find a place she belongs in a world of face masks and silence. She currently has one book out, a poetic autobiography called "Soul Survivor" and is hard at work on her second. Follow her at facebook.com/mandyspoetry and @kocsismandy on Instagram

LEIGH ALISON

Leigh Alison has lived on three continents (so far) in her lifetime. She was born in Zimbabwe, grew up in South Africa, spent two years in the UK, and now lives in Massachusetts USA. Needless to say, her Gypsy Soul loves exploring new places and traveling. She is one of those people that feels like she expresses herself best through the written word and she began writing in 2012. When she's not working as a Registered Nurse, or writing, she loves spending time with her two sons, the Love of her Life, and a menagerie of pets (she has five cats and a dog… for now). To read more of her writing, you can find her at facebook.com/FlameLilyPoetry | instagram.com/flamelilypoetry

GYPSY'S REVERIE

Gypsy's Reverie is a woman who considers herself to be a free spirit, wandering far off the beaten path and following her wild heart in relentless pursuit of passion and an authentic life. Her writing tells the tale of her struggle to climb out of the dark abyss and back into the light--finding her truth and herself again after years of feeling broken and lost. Always a lover of words and stories, she began writing to help herself heal and to chronicle her process of becoming. Gypsy's Reverie is so thankful to be able to share her journey on the road less traveled with other wandering souls through her words. It is her hope that her writing may serve to encourage, inspire, and/or amuse you while you travel through this life.
facebook.com/ascended.from.ashes | instagram.com/gypsysreverie/

SPENSER SPELLMEYER

Spenser Spellmeyer is a young up and coming writer. Spenser penned his first poetry piece in 2019 to help him make sense of his grief from the loss of his father at a young age. Even though Spenser is young, his writing is mature, powerful and soul piercing. Spenser is a high school student who enjoys history, video games, music, reading Edgar Allan Poe and spending time with his family. Spenser has been published as a Spotlight Writer in the book Scars of a Warrior and part of the anthology Rise From Within. You can follow Spenser's poetry on Facebook. facebook.com/spenserroyalspelly

T H SMART

T H Smart is a writer, poet, and visual storyteller. Both creative and strategic, she is as comfortable in the boardroom and training room, as she is in her home studio creating visual and written art. She weaves the threads of inspiration she collects in life and work into her writing. By sharing the beautiful messages that skewer her heart, she hopes to stir up others in love so they might be strengthened and inspired to run after the plans and purposes for their lives. She shares her suburban home in Cape Town, South Africa with her husband, daughter, and four furry friends. You can find more of her writing on her website Warrior for Worthiness (www.warriorforworthiness) as well as her Smart Musings on Facebook (facebook.com/SmartMuser/), Instagram (instagram.com/thsmart_smartmuser/) or LinkedIn (linkedin.com/in/thsmart/).

S.A. QUINOX

S.A. Quinox is a young, Belgian poet who writes for the aching, the yearning and the mad wanderers among us. She loves to write about the dark night of the soul. The parts that we so desperately try to keep hidden. Quinox can be found on social media through Facebook and Instagram. facebook.com/SAQuinoxPoetry | teespring.com/stores/quinox-poetry

JUMPED UP

Diana Lynn Thomas started writing short stories and poetry following a traumatic brain injury at age 66. She writes under the pseudonyms of Jumped Up and TenderMercies. She has contributed her poetry to three publications: (1) "Star Wishes" in Thoughts and Prayers - A collection of poetic inspiration; in which all proceeds go to the Children's Cancer Foundation; (2) "Dawn's Eternal Journey" in The Chosen One - Volume 1 - India Press/Creative Writing Modern Age, and (3) Various Poetry and Prose in The Chosen One - Volume 2 - India Press/Creative Writing Modern Age. Diana explains her writings as an awakening of random thoughts and long buried life traumas. She says she writes for those unable to speak their own truths. To be their voice and their advocate for in her words, "unspoken words are the saddest of all things we carry within us". Please venture into her worlds of truth, hope, fantasy, and sometimes despair. - facebook.com/dianajumpedup

CLINT DAVIS

Clint Davis is a former Paramedic who has seen tragedy and triumphs up close and personal. He can thrive in the dark but finds joy in the light. He lives for a laugh and dies when he cries. He believes in love but always drives it away. He loves humanity but hates people. He always adapts but never fits in. He wants world peace but would be fine with an apocalypse. Basically, he's complicated. More of Clint's writing can be found on Facebook at facebook.com/RoninDraygun/

MARY O'CONNELL LOTERBAUER (MEL)

Poetry is timeless and universal. It has the power to make people laugh, cry, and heal. I have always been terrified to allow people to read the emotions I had spilled onto paper as it was like standing before them naked in the cold, baring my soul. Taking the plunge and allowing it to be seen by others is not an easy task, but necessary for this leg of my life journey. I have found that the darkness we face inside needs to be surrendered to discover your light. My writing is my white flag of surrender. If you really want to know someone, ask them to share with you their favorite poems or even music lyrics. It reveals who they are, where they have been, and where they want to go. One day I hope my name gets shared when you are asked what healed you. - facebook.com/profile.php?id=100069760041325

SARAH HALL

Sarah Hall is an indie writer and resides in Adelaide, Australia. She is 43 years of age and has been writing poetry and prose for several years. Sarah is the owner and sole writer at Sarah's Collection of Scar's on Facebook with plans to release her own collection of work this coming year. Sarah is a featured author in the "Rise From Within" poetry anthology by 300 South Media group and has been involved with judging and editing Rise Up Rabid Souls with Ship Street Poetry. Sarah writes powerful, emotive, raw and sometimes dark pieces. Her works are often inspired by her survival of domestic violence and other personal experiences in life, love and loss. facebook.com/sarahscollectionofscars

APRIL SPELLMEYER

April Spellmeyer began to write when she lost her husband in 2011. When April penned her first piece of poetry the floodgates opened up about loss, grief, mental illness and trauma. While April expresses in raw, unfiltered emotional imagery she balances it with the beauty of hope, love, strength and healing. April finds several genres of music brings her words to life to tattoo them on the world. April is the mother to four children, three fur babies and Gigi to three grandsons. April enjoys reading, history, Star Wars and enjoying time with her family. April is the co-author of Soul Words - Eternal Soul Sisters Volume I, author of They Call Me Sister Kate, Sacrifice & Bloom, Scars of a Warrior and Poetry Stained Lips. You can find her books on Amazon Follow her on Facebook at facebook.com/aprilyspellmeyer and on Facebook and Instagram at Eternal Soul Sisters.

BRANDIE WHALEY

Brandie Whaley is a long-time resident of Myrtle Beach South Carolina. She is a proud single mother of two boys, Sean, who turned 27 on the 11th of July, and Caleb, who will be 23 on the 4th of March. She has been writing for pleasure since her early teen years and has always had a passion for the written word. Brandie has struggled with actuve addiction for the majority of her adult life, and has lost many lives to their own battles with addiction. She honors those lost with some of her writings and acknowledges her own fight with it in many of her poems. If you'd like to read more you can follow her on facebook at : facebook.com/thewordsiliveby

ASHLEY NICOLSON

Ashley resides in North Dakota surrounded by family and friends. She dedicates the majority of her time to helping those in need to heal and overcome by finding the beauty and humor in life.

KATHLEEN SCHLOMER

Kathleen Schlomer is a 17 year old artist and writer who resides in North Dakota. She began writing poetry at 13 years old as a way to work through emotional trauma and the events the world would throw her way. She spends every day reminding everyone to keep fighting, regardless of the circumstances you find yourself in.

BRIAN BERRYMAN

Brian Berryman was born and raised in Abington Massachusetts, and lives near there to this day. He is new to writing, having started in the summer of 2020. A former auto mechanic who transitioned to IT almost twenty years ago, he works in IT support for a community health care center in Boston. When he is not writing, Brian enjoys spending time with his fiancée Leigh and her two sons, playing guitar, singing karaoke, British sit-coms, and exploring Antique Stores. facebook.com/FlameLilyPoetry | instagram.com/flamelilypoetry/

EMMA GLEDHILL

"I feel as though a love of words, stories and books have been a part of me all my life. Books have always been a sanctuary." Emma tends to lean towards a more melancholy subject matter. She began to write, as an adult, after the end of a marriage that she felt she had to escape from rather than end. Writing, mostly indirectly, about the experience and the person she has become since, became a cathartic exercise. Coupling that with finding the man that is the other half to her soul gave her a well of emotion and perspective Emma often draws upon. Being a happily married mother of two small children doesn't always allow her the time to write as she wishes but she wouldn't change that. However it is why it means so much to her to have been chosen to participate in this anthology. Follow her on Facebook at facebook.com/PentoPaperC2G

T H SMART

T H Smart is a writer, poet, visual storyteller, and all-round creative spirit. Both creative and strategic, she is as comfortable in the boardroom and training room, as she is in her home studio creating visual and written art. She weaves the threads of inspiration she collects in life and work through her writing. By sharing the beautiful messages that skewer her heart, she hopes to stir up others in love so they might be strengthened and inspired to run after the plans and purposes for their lives. She shares her suburban home in Cape Town, South Africa with her husband, daughter, and four furry friends. You can find more of her writing on facebook.com/smartmuser, Instagram (tarynhaynessmart) & her website (warriorforworthiness.co.za)

AVANT AVANT-GARDE

Avant is a profuse lover of words—words, the saving grace and the hellfire of how she draws breath; the only spoken her soul is literate in. Inspired at an early age by the Classic poets that have paved the way for us to embrace calligraphy of the soul, her page, Avant-Avant-garde, and several others I write for-- Black & Gold Poetry Page etc... are dedicated to being an advocate for writers of all levels across various social media platforms and published work. facebook.com/SavantAvantGarde

MARGIE WATTS

Margie grew up in the Eastern Coastal area part of Georgia known as the Golden Isles. She loved it there, living near the ocean. Even as a child she loved looking out past the horizon. It felt like looking at forever. Walking, sand between her toes and picking up seashells. Just her and her shadow. "Me time", she called it. Butterflies was another of her favorites. Their beauty as they flew around. How they start out in the darkness of a cocoon and find their way out into the light as a beautiful butterfly. A reminder that darkness is not always a bad thing. There can be beauty from darkness. She was always an avid reader and a constant dreamer. Her debut book Wounded Butterfly was released in 2020-she never dreamed that all the tidbits on scraps of paper, notebooks filled with writings, would lead her to her dream of becoming an author. Follow her on Facebook at facebook.com/reflectionsofawoundedbutterfly

CRISTINA LANE

Cristina Lane is making her poetry debut in this anthology. She resides in the Midwest, and has returned to her roots in her hometown of Sweet Springs. She draws inspiration from life experiences in her writings. She also finds her peace by gardening, listening to good music, and spending time playing in the garden.
instagram.com/cristina_a_lane

TABASSUM H

Tabassum Hasnat, a freelance writer of shortform fictitious genres, currently completing her IALs under Pearson Edexcel along with law and legal studies. She has co authored multiple international book compilations and anthologies published on platforms like Amazon, Kindle, Google books, Kobo, Barnes & Nobles, Notion Press. At the moment, she's working as an intern for Quirky Magazine and as content executive for an Art centric organization named Esscre. Follow her on Facebook at facebook.com/tabassum.hasnat.10 and @_tashaa8055_ on Instagram

NICOLE CARLYON

I am a sensitive soul, a day dreamer, dabbling in random words as a form of escape from a past that eludes me. I write to help me heal, and hope that in doing so I can touch others and make them feel less alone in a world that doesn't always make sense. Raw and real the words that flow come from my soul and I do not apologise for being me (although I am still on a journey to find out who she is). My promise to myself is that I will keep writing until I find her or until the words run dry and I have nothing left to give. instagram.com/nicolecarylon | facebook.com/HerDestinyDreamsandDesires | facebook.com/freetobesoulsensitive

JAY LONG

Jay Long is a New York based author, poet, and natural storyteller. His creative voice can be heard throughout social media and online writing communities. Through his writing and work with other writers, he continues to establish himself as one of today's prolific voices. To learn more about Jay visit jaylongwrites.com or you can follow him on Facebook at facebook.com/writerjaylong and @writerjaylong on Instagram

EVA COFFEY

Eva Coffey, a cheesy romantic coffee lover, always has an obsession with words. She writes from her heart about things that matters like faith and love. While grief is a lonely dark place, she hopes her words can offer some kind of solace to the ones who need them. She can be found at coffeylovenook.com | facebook.com/coffeylovenook

PT MULDOON

PT Muldoon is a Michigan based father, husband, rancher, and writer. His first book is available now on Amazon. To follow PT Muldoon check out ptmuldoon.com | facebook.com/PTMuldoonPoetry

JANA BEGOVIC

As far back as she can remember, Jana has been fascinated by storytelling. Her love of reading and writing propelled her toward studies of languages and literature. Among her publications are academic articles, the novel Poisonous Whispers, Roane Publishing, N.Y., poetry, short fiction, articles, art reviews, and blog posts featured in various literary journals. She is a senior editor at Ariel Chart, and a contributing editor for Canada Fashion Magazine. She has been nominated for the 2019 Best of the Net and the PushCart awards. She can be contacted via her Author Page at facebook.com/J.Damselfly/

JAMIE SANTOMASSO

Jamie Santomasso is an author from Kansas City, Mo. A writer since the age of five, she has used the literary arts as a means to express her thoughts and feelings through the written word. Follow her at facebook.com/spiritofthesonneteer

JERILYN SCAVO REED

She first started writing poetry almost 30 years ago, in the fourth grade; encouraged by a teacher, Sister Marylou. Through the years, Jerilyn has utilized poetry as a creative and therapeutic outlet of processing and self-expression. As her style continues to develop, she finds herself looking to capture darker themes, follow a more unique rhythm and flow; without constant rhyming, and utilize punctuation while capturing off-beats. Jerilyn finds herself wanting to share her poetry more as she grows older. She hopes that when people read her words, they can follow her beat, feel her heat, and are hopefully touched and perhaps slightly uncomfortable or disturbed. Jerilyn's passion is boundless and endless. Instagram.com/jjreed81 | On Facebook Jerilyn Scavo Reed

JAI K

Jai K is an an author, poet and traveler who lives in Nashville, Tennessee. She is a lifetime creative whose work has appeared in Pennsylvania English, Penman Review, Where the Mind Dwells, Literary Yard, Georgia's Best Emerging Poets 2017, The Evening Street Press, America's Emerging Poets 2018: Southeast Region, Route 7, Birmingham Arts Journal, Backchannels Journal, Hive Avenue Literary Journal, and was also accepted for publication in the Sandy River Review. Follow Jai K at facebook.com/JaiK8282 | instagram.com/jai_k82

SHAUNA WOODBURY

Shauna was born in Calgary Alberta Canada. She writes, plays baseball, loves beer and festivals. She writes from a darker side but loves the rainbow fireworks the little happy moments in life bring. She has two sons and a beautiful life partner to complete her world. Her future endeavours hope to include more writing, more living, and brighter connections. At the age of 50 her life and literary creations are just beginning. Join her on her journey. https://www.facebook.com/SexLeatherHearts

ABOUT 300 SOUTH MEDIA GROUP

300 South's founder, Jay Long, saw a lack of one-on-one interaction for those seeking assistance when self-publishing their books. He noticed far too much misinformation being made readily available to would-be authors and companies trying to capitalize on the trust of inexperienced self-publishers.

300 South was begun with the hope to level the playing field for indie writers and authors. For far too long self-published authors were considered hacks – and that is because many self-published books didn't take on a professional look or feel. Whether that was from lack of knowledge and understanding or not truly identifying the full scope of what goes into a successful self-published project. Jay wanted to offer helpful solutions for indie authors stepping into the public spotlight.

The heart and soul of the company is its dedication to providing indie authors with information and services to help ensure their projects are top quality and ready for your readers.

The vision of 300 South is to guide and mentor determined writers towards the goal of being self-published. We assist you to find the best course of action to achieve your goals. Our services help ensure you put out quality, professional products to the world.

Visit 300 South Media Group online
Website-300smg.com
Facebook & Instagram-300SouthPublishing
Twitter-300SouthMedia

MORE FROM 300 SOUTH MEDIA GROUP

ANTHOLOGIES

RISE FROM WITHIN
SUNSET RAIN

AUTHORS

SEASONS OF A SEWER GIRL by DAWN P. HARRELL
POETRY STAINED LIPS by APRIL Y. SPELLMEYER
TIMELESS CHATTER by JAY LONG
ETERNAL ECHOES by JAY LONG

UPCOMING RELEASES

INSIDE THESE WALLS by EMILY JAMES
SHE'S MAGIC & MIDNIGHT LACE by ANN MARIE ELEAZER
REFLECTIONS OF ME by MARGIE WATTS
IN PIECES by JAY LONG

For more information on these or any upcoming releases, please bookmark the future home of 300 SOUTH PUBLISHING on the web 300southpublishing.com

Made in the USA
Middletown, DE
06 August 2021